I am Your Neighbor

Voices from a Chicago Food Pantry

David R. Brown and Roger Wright

ISBN: 1475250371
ISBN 13: 9781475250374

TABLE OF CONTENTS

Personal Notes from the Authors vii
Acknowledgments.. xix

YOUR NEIGHBORS

Introduction: To Give People a Voice 1
Danny: *Mixing the Pot*... 14
Cheryl: *Question Mark* 27
Ernie: *A Work in Progress* 34
Angelina: *Gems* 45
Wayne: *An American Spirit*.. 51
Leonora: *The Chemistry Professor*................................. 65
James: *Doing Something Good in Life* 73
Carl: *The Actor* 86
Marie: *Rainbow Lady*... 98
Tom: *A Working Man*.. 107
Lauren: *From the Neighborhood* 132
Raymond: *Serving His Country*................................... 143
Susan: *One Wish* 150
Carlos: *A Married Man* 156
Dave: *Playing Rough* 168
Gerald: *His Moment* 180
Len: *Angels in Disguise* 187
Elvia: *A Faithful Woman* 201
Rosie: *The Grateful* 208
Flora: *There Is No Book for This*.................................. 214
Dennis: *The Buildings* 221
Circles of Leadership 227

APPENDIX

Common Pantry 242
Greater Chicago Food Depository................................. 244
Feeding America 246

Personal Notes from the Authors
DAVID R. BROWN

Throughout my life I have always been drawn to and motivated by underdogs.

Underdogs – those people who seem to have the odds stacked against them, yet continue their daily struggle with a dream of being "normal" or "average." Simply doing the best they can to provide a living for themselves and/or their families. Whether their underdog status was self-inflicted, coincidental or situational never really mattered to me. Just the fact that the day ahead of them was going to be filled with more and different struggles than mine, made my heart swell from an early age. My affinity with underdogs even included being a Cleveland Browns fan in the 1970's and 1980's with heartbreaking losses only serving to galvanize my support and pride in the team. Today I am a Chicago Cubs fan.

On the flip side, I have also found myself driven to action when I encounter people who have no real appreciation for underdogs, fail to empathize with them in any way and even revel in blaming them for their lot in life.

I was born in Grove City, Ohio into a middle-class family of privilege. While money was *not* one of those privileges, I was blessed to grow up with the love and support of my family, friends, good public schools, sports, music and church. Our family struggled financially and we faced our share of tragedy and misfortune, but I grew up always thinking our lives were perfect. We didn't have much and didn't feel we needed much. My brothers, sisters and I never had a long list of presents we wanted for Christmas or birthdays.

The privileges at my family's disposal to deal with difficult circumstances in our life were the right combinations of support and independence, pride and humility, tears and laughter. We also understood that no matter how bad our situation, there were always others in our community, or on the other side of the world, who were struggling just a bit more and could use our help. We grew up in a culture of frequent volunteering and charitable work and, in turn, enjoyed a great support network ourselves. When schools and church had food drives or fundraisers for less fortunate families we always participated with great enthusiasm.

I have lived in Chicago since my escape from ten exciting and rewarding years living in New York City and was quickly drawn to volunteer at the Common Pantry initially as a result of my membership at Epiphany United Church of Christ and my desire to get involved in my new community. It was rewarding being part of an organization doing great things for hundreds of families in our neighborhood every week. My motivation was strong and passionate.

As you will read in this book, some of this volunteer activity evolved into being one of the spokesmen for Common Pantry when called to meetings with the alderman and concerned neighbors. Little did I know that my encounters with people who were a threat to our organization would push my passion for Common Pantry to another level.

I was diagnosed with cancer in May 2008. Following chemotherapy and as I continued my recovery the next year, I was able to allocate even more time to volunteering. This continues today, including a few hours each Wednesday afternoon when I don a neon-colored "Security" vest to greet clients and stroll the alleys and surrounding blocks to assure our neighbors that all is quiet on the Pantry front. This has also given me a wonderful opportunity to spend more one-on-one time with clients just getting to know them and understand their lives a bit better.

I came up with the idea for this book when it became clear to me that the best way to combat opposition from concerned neighbors was to share with them the real stories of these real people who are their neighbors. I knew immediately that Roger Wright was the perfect person with whom to collaborate on this project, given his passion for writing, love of the great Chicago authors and storytellers like Studs Terkel and his easy conversational manner for leading the interviews with our clients at Common Pantry.

I am so thankful for the opportunity to have coordinated this project, for the stories shared and for the connections made amongst neighbors to make all of our lives a little bit better each day.

David R. Brown, Chicago — May 2012

DAVID R. BROWN: BIOGRAPHY

David R. Brown has been a commercial real estate professional his entire 26 year career. *"I am Your Neighbor"* is his first book, never having the urge to author any guides on how to make money in real estate with no money down.

Prior jobs at international real estate companies took him on grueling business trips to many places around the globe including London, Paris, Munich, Cannes, Frankfurt, Berlin, Prague, Zurich, Sydney, Melbourne, Hong Kong, Tokyo and Singapore. David now enjoys a much more local focus with the challenges and rewards of running his own company doing property advisory, investment, development and finance.

His true passion is his family and his community, spending time at sporting events, plays and dance recitals and in meetings with the school board, church, Common Pantry, community groups and other non-profit organizations.

David is a native of Grove City, Ohio. Following his college years in Evanston and Cambridge, David lived in New York City for ten years before returning to Chicago to settle down in 1995. He and his wife Shannon have two young daughters, Stella and Hazel.

David is a graduate of Richard Avenue Elementary School, Brookpark Middle School and Grove City High School. He is also a graduate of Northwestern University with a BA in Urban

Studies and Political Science, and received his Master of Public Policy from Harvard's Kennedy School of Government with a concentration in Housing and Community Development. He continues to learn something new every day that was not covered in school.

ROGER WRIGHT

What brings me here? It's you. It's anyone reading these words.

What brings me here is a belief about something that happened a really long time ago. It happened about 30 seconds after our common ancestor crawled out of the oceans or mud, stood up on two feet for the very first time, took a look around, and noticed another human-like creature. Now I can't be sure. But I can believe that one of the first things that this one neighbor said to the other was, "Have I got a story for you."

I believe that the human urge to tell one's story is as universal as blood.

We can call it oral history, blogging, reporting, case study, fact or fiction. But in the end, it's telling a story. It's almost like an instinct. An instinct that connects all of us.

That universal connection means that no one is left out. Best part of this story telling instinct is that it includes all of us. Everyone is welcome.

It has never been a secret that the story of the normal, everyday person can be even more compelling than tales of kings and princes. But Studs Terkel brought that truism alive like no one else ever had before.

Studs inspired us.

He knew how to get out of the way and let the story come through. He listened with a fierce intensity. He captured the high notes in a person's story and shaped them into a song. Is that "writing?" You could call it that. But it's more. It's writing that can be perfectly suited for a team.

And David Brown was the ideal partner in this team. His big heart, razor sharp mind, and the fact that he does what he says he will do, crystallized our common goals at the start. He named the book and I instantaneously nodded "Yes!" He engaged the Board of the Common Pantry and other supporters along the way. He and I were partners every step of the process.

The team was joined by a whole host of people recognized in the acknowledgements. All of us in celebration of the stories shared in this book.

The act of story telling is like a golden thread that binds all of us. When I can listen to a story, I feel like I just might belong to something larger than myself. And in belonging, I feel included. That's what brings me here. I feel included.

But there's a second reason I'm here. The second reason is "mystery."

There are elements of mystery in every single story. The mystery might be that something is missing from the story. You find yourself thinking, "Then what happened?" Perhaps somebody says something that does not make sense to you. You read a passage and think, "This is not what I expected to hear." Mystery abounds in this book.

And it's these mysteries that prompt me to think. To reach for the things I don't know. To start with something I don't understand, something that is a mystery, and then try to figure it out. To perhaps think differently. To learn. And that journey of learning is a spirit that helps me feel alive.

So what brings me here is the drive to feel included. And then it's the learning that starts with mystery and makes me feel alive.

Finally, it's the fact that I'm a neighbor too.

If you read this book and like it, that will be great. If you read it and want to help the Common Pantry, that will be even better. But if you also read the book and recognize the unique ways that you too are a neighbor, then you will have heard exactly what all of us who worked on the book are trying with all our might to say.

A universal voice saying one simple but infinitely rich statement.

"I am your neighbor."

Roger Wright, Chicago - May 2012

ROGER WRIGHT: BIOGRAPHY

Roger Wright, a Chicago native, has been writing since he could hold a pencil.

His early work life was as a Special Education Teacher in the Uptown Neighborhood of Chicago and in starting the Education and Workforce Development Program for Jobs For Youth Chicago.

He is a former ghostwriter, training developer and speaker for Gallup Publishing and has 20 years of experience in writing and leading customer service, management and leadership development programs in business, non-profit, education and faith settings. His "Chicago Guy" blog has a worldwide readership and has been a regular feature on-line at www.Fictionique.com and, for the past four years, the blog aggregator Open Salon. His upcoming book titles are: "Finding Work When There Are No Jobs" (Publication Date: January 2013) and "Street Corner Spirits."

Roger is a graduate of Beloit College and Players Workshop of The Second City.

ACKNOWLEDGEMENTS

DEDICATIONS

FROM DAVID -

To my late father, Richard V. Brown, who could share stories to match the ones in this book.

To my wonderful mom, Claudette Brown, who loves every day of the life she was given.

To my lovely wife, Shannon, who dislikes personal recognition and acknowledgements, but thank you.

To my daughters Stella and Hazel who I know will live interesting lives, share their gifts and touch other lives with their compassion.

FROM ROGER -

To Maria. And our family of all shapes and sizes.

INDIVIDUALS WHO HELPED WITH THIS BOOK IN MANY WAYS:

Vanessa Bechtel

Scott Best

Rebecca Bodner

Bethany Bohn

Claudette Brown

Carolyn Bull

Kelly Daly

Matthew S. Diener

Holly Dwyer

Kathy Engert

Ericka Foster

Suzanne Geier

Nancy Guigle

Julie Hobert

Karen Kouf

Linnette Mathys

Colleen Oliver

Elizabeth Press

Matilde Trujillo

Jessy Williams

Desiree Winkle

BUSINESSES AND ORGANIZATIONS
THAT HAVE SUPPORTED THIS PROJECT:

Angel Food Bakery

Apart Pizza

Architectural Artifacts

The Bad Apple

Café 28

City Provisions

Feeding America

Fountainhead

Greater Chicago Food Depository

Half Acre Beer Company

Metropolitan Brewing Company

Mission Printing

Real Kitchen

Rusty Cut

Spacca Napoli Pizzeria

Starbucks

VineJoy

Volo Restaurant and Wine Bar

West Lakeview Liquors

INTRODUCTION

———

To Give People a Voice

"Alkies, crackheads and gangbangers."

That's what they've been called. It's been shouted with anger and disgust in public meetings; whispered in private conversations; snarled and spit out like a weapon by some of the people who share a neighborhood with them on the north side of Chicago.

"Alkies, crackheads and gangbangers."

Sometimes the description was translated more politely: *"They're just different. They're not like us."*

Whether the talk was public or private, civil or hateful, "these people" lining up for food outside the Common Pantry, Chicago's oldest continuously running food pantry, made people nervous. And I understood that. I try my best to see both sides of any issue. There were legitimate concerns here: security; cleanliness; property values. I understood.

These were not the people lining up on Chicago's North Michigan Avenue at the Apple Store hungry for the newest iPhone. These were not the people in the daily line at Hot Doug's to get the best in "encased meats." The lines wrapped around the blocks at *those* establishments caused no fear, except with their competition.

1

The people in the line at the Common Pantry weren't always dressed nicely. They might have looked a little worn down. As a group, they represented more of a colorful cross section of our society.

From a distance, the clients of the Common Pantry were just nameless, faceless people lining up on Damen Avenue to get some free food, some healthy food options for their families to tide them over in a month that had seen a job loss, an illness, a family tragedy.

Seeing these strangers come to the doors of the Common Pantry each Wednesday and line up in the bitter freezing winds of a January snow or in the sweltering heat of a humid Chicago summer made lots of people nervous.

And again, I understood that.

This nervousness prompted the local alderman to summon those of us in leadership roles at the Common Pantry to attend meetings with neighbors many times over the past several years. Our task was to answer complaints received by the local alderman from a small group of his constituents.

On their side of the discussion was nervous anger and fear.

On our side of the discussion was the simple desire to feed hungry neighbors. We were a group of patient, dedicated volunteers with a passion for social justice who was perceived by some as a naïve group of "do-gooders."

At the beginning, fear usually won out.

The people who complained to the alderman made it clear that they wanted the Common Pantry gone from the neighborhood. We tried to make it clear that the people we served were also their neighbors, that a real need existed, and that we were there to stay. They requested wholesale changes to the operations of the Common Pantry, like moving the entrance out of their sight to the opposite corner of the building. We refused since it was obvious a change like this would negatively impact our clients and operations. Instead, we proposed a series of incremental changes that addressed every one of the complaints against us while enhancing our clients' experience.

We won small victories for the Common Pantry, like insisting that the folks we fed were referred to as "clients" or simply "neighbors in need" instead of the nasty labels that rolled so easily off the tongues on the other side of the table.

Those initial meetings arranged by the alderman were filled with tension and occasional personal verbal attacks. We tried our best to diffuse the tension and calm the fear. We knew that fear was most potent when there was no name, no voice, no real known person serving to prompt that fear. Fear was most terrifying when the source was, in fact, without a voice.

That is why we wrote this book.

To give these wonderful people, the clients of the Common Pantry, a voice.

The stories included in this book and many other stories will continue every week on our corner of the world because of the overwhelming support we enjoy from the majority of neighbors, businesses, schools and churches who answer the call to help our neighbors in need. Unlike the first meeting called by the alderman to give a voice to the concerned neighbors when we felt besieged, the final meeting demonstrated overwhelming community support as the room gradually filled beyond capacity with Common Pantry supporters (many recognizable to the alderman and his staff as well-regarded community leaders) outnumbering the others 80 to 2.

This book was never intended to be a collection of woeful tales, a coffee-table book showing the worn faces of hard lives, or a complete documentation of a life's progression and how a place like the Common Pantry can help turn things around. The real measure of how the Common Pantry can change a life isn't found in descriptive prose, facts and figures on the Common Pantry as an institution. The real measure, the real story is found in the voices of the clients of the Common Pantry telling their stories. The voices of the clients tell not just how the pantry helped them; they get at why the Common Pantry is here.

Every single story speaks directly from the heart of a living and breathing person in our neighborhood who has been fed, — often in more ways than you would imagine, —by the Common Pantry. These are personal stories, told by hungry, struggling people in their own words. The success of the Common Pantry is heard in the voices of real people that many of us now call friends.

When interviewing clients for this book, we made it a point not to ask them only about their hunger and their struggles, although these struggles are what bind them together on

Wednesdays at the Common Pantry. These stories are snapshots of the stories that clients chose to share with us on that one particular day they were given a voice and encouraged to use that voice in whatever way they chose.

We hope you can leave your expectations behind and let our neighbors share their stories with you. We think that what you'll find here is the same thing you'll find with any neighbors: every single person here is an individual. Simplistic "explanations" of hardship and despair don't scratch the surface of what you'll get in listening hard and deep.

The authors of this book are not academics conducting research into the root causes of poverty, homelessness and hunger. We have not done any statistical analyses or sophisticated tabulations or correlations. We are obviously interested in learning more about these root causes, but our research "methodology" was simply to listen to what our neighbors, these Common Pantry clients, had to say.

Statistics, graphs and tables can contribute to the dehumanizing of a very personal issue. The stories you are about to read will let you draw your own graphs, come up with your own correlations and think creatively about new ways to help your neighbors who happen to be struggling. While some of the people telling their stories on these pages might be sharing experiences foreign to you, others will be very familiar.

You will find common threads that run through the stories, including:

- Unexpected illness or death of a family member
- Job loss and economic distress
- Feelings of being "different" and not fitting in
- Romantic struggles
- Long-held feelings of regret
- Chemical dependency
- Depression and anxiety

You may have had similar struggles in your own life. You may recognize the misfortune of having more than one of these events occur simultaneously. Perhaps you may conclude that the only thing separating you from the folks at the Common Pantry is your stronger network of support——or pure luck.

Turning on the Tape Recorder
and Making the Client Comfortable

What you will *not* find here are stories with contrived messages. Nor will you find stories tailored to counter negative stereotypes or respond to what we thought were unfair attacks on clients.

Our approach was to turn on the tape recorder and do whatever we could to make the clients comfortable in telling the stories that were important to them.

The style and spirit of this book sits squarely in the tradition of Studs Terkel, the late Chicago author and historian. While there will never be another Studs Terkel, the heart of his work—a belief that the real stories of "ordinary" people shine the brightest light on our common humanity—lives on.

We expect that most readers who read and listen to every story will give the book a "mixed review." You will hear from people to whom you are immediately drawn and about whom you want to know more; there will be others that you don't really care for too much. It will be kind of like your own neighborhood—or any neighborhood, anywhere.

As a backdrop to these stories, you'll be graced with eyewitness accounts of Chicago history touching on prohibition, politics, race, crime and social mores of the 1950s, 1960s and 1970s. These are the stories of our times. You will hear our friends from the Common Pantry recall some of Chicago's past including reactions to Martin Luther King's marches in Chicago, the 1968 Democratic Convention and subsequent riots, visits to Riverview Amusement Park, the changing racial mix in public housing, and how the headline events of their childhood impacted their lives.

This book would not have been possible without the Common Pantry Board's support, underwritten by a private donation to the Common Pantry providing that 100 percent of net sales revenue benefits Common Pantry.

The Common Pantry —Addressing Food Insecurity

The historical roots of the Common Pantry first took hold in an organization called the North Side Cooperative Ministry (NSCM) that was in existence from 1962 to 1972. The NSCM was a visionary organization that initiated Christian mission work throughout Chicago's North Side.

Mirroring the turbulence of social change in the 1960s, the array of societal needs and inter-organizational struggles, the NSCM emerged with an impressive list of initiatives including:

- Legal advice clinics
- Citizen health clinics
- Day care alliance
- Neighborhood development corporation
- North side women's center

A central initiative was the North Side Community Pantries, which had locations in three Lincoln Park churches. The Pantries began operation in 1967 and eventually merged into the Common Pantry. With historical roots going back to 1967, the Common Pantry is the longest continually operating food pantry in Chicago. In 1983, the Common Pantry established its current home when it rented space in a corner of the basement at Epiphany United Church of Christ (UCC) with a separate address of 3744 N. Damen Avenue.

Epiphany UCC is a vibrant urban church with a proud history of advocacy for social justice, consistent with the UCC founding principles. While Common Pantry and Epiphany United Church of Christ enjoy a special collaborative relationship, and serve many of the same people in different ways, they are two distinct organizations with separate missions, bylaws, leadership, funding sources, expense budgets, etc.

At the start of 2003, Epiphany church members were focused on the fact that their church doors were opening up each Wednesday to scores of hungry neighbors. A handful of families initiated a Welcome Meal at 6:00 p.m. each Wednesday to provide a dignified, hot meal and a sense of community to these neighbors while they were at the church to pick up their groceries. The meal was initially cooked by the church members in the basement kitchen or at their homes, but now the dinners are full gourmet-catered meals provided by First Slice, an organization whose mission is to provide access to wholesome food for those living in poverty.

In 2009, Epiphany's Fellowship Hall was opened up as "Common Community" - a Wednesday afternoon community center for Common Pantry clients, supported financially by members of the church pursuing a mission of social justice that need not venture out to seek those in need, but may simply answer the knocks on the door.

Expanding the services on Wednesday afternoons was a milestone in the history of the Common Pantry. While the opening of Fellowship Hall was originally done to eliminate the lines of people waiting outside the Pantry door, it also set the stage for the Common Pantry to become a social center in collaboration with Epiphany Church. Throughout the book, you will see just what that has meant in the lives of both clients and those we serve at the

Common Pantry We are now very proud to announce that as "I am Your Neighbor" goes to press, this Wednesday afternoon program has, in fact, been taken under the umbrella of Common Pantry and is now officially known as "Common Community."

Other improvements were made in the operation of the Common Pantry from 2008 to 2012 as the challenges to the survival of the institution mirrored the challenges in serving those most vulnerable across the world:

- Expanded the waiting area inside to accommodate an additional 15 seats
- Hired a security guard, to patrol the sidewalks and alleys while also greeting and assisting clients and volunteers
- Improved collaboration with Epiphany UCC and the Wednesday evening "Welcome Meal"
- Initiated a Fresh Produce Mobile with Greater Chicago Food Depository for an additional day of food distribution on Mondays

From Food Distribution to Holistic Solutions

Wiping out hunger in America is an ambitious—some say impossible—goal. A more achievable goal is to address the needs of the vulnerable. This means respecting our neighbors, not just through food distribution, but with the holistic approach of trying to help people build better lives, one person at a time, day by day.

Through our expanded services offered through "Common Community"—with improved linkages to social service agencies and compassionate people with laptop computers to assist with housing options for previously homeless people—we were able to help a great deal more. We learned, however, that just like a bag of free groceries every month won't solve the problem of hunger or poverty, giving a homeless person a furnished apartment doesn't completely solve the housing problem either.

Holistic solutions must be attempted but little successes must be celebrated. As nice as it would be to change the world, our focus is this corner of the globe on the north side of Chicago. Even this corner has immense needs, and some of these will never be met. What we can do is make just part of one person's day better while showing them respect and a smile or two. We can also just listen when the rest of the world does not.

That's what we did in this book. We listened. And we invite you to do the same.

DANNY
Mixing the Pot

———

Danny expends more energy sitting in a chair than most people do running a mile. He's a big man, in his 50s with a winning smile and the energy of a person 20 years his junior. Danny uses his hands to frame chunks of information, like invisible building blocks, from which he'll build his story. He is a survivor. He is also a thinker and a leader.

At 17, Danny led a gang of 200 guys, one that included kids of every race and color. Danny says, "So we were like a big old pot. We had beans, corn, Chinese food, everything. We were all trying to get to know each other. Mixing the pot. And that was how it started."

———

There's so many chapters in my life. We're not gonna get to all of them.

I'm just gonna give you the chapter on the projects. Yeah. The projects. Let's start there.

Chapter One. I was born in 1956. In Lathrop Homes. The only mixed projects in the City of Chicago. We're at Diversey, Clybourn and Damen. Right on the Chicago River.

At first, there were only four Black families. We were one of four black families. For years and years. Starting in 1956 to the early 60s. Then they started throwing in more blacks.

Our friends were old white ladies. Because there were no kids. So we'd talk to the old ladies. They couldn't play, but they could talk.

We went to the store for them. And we bought two things for those old ladies. Cottage cheese and milk. They sent us to the store with a quarter and we brought them back cottage cheese and milk. We got to keep the leftover money. Now in those days, a quarter was a lot of money. You could get 75 pieces of candy for a quarter. Three pieces of candy for a penny. All you need is one quarter. You're straight. So we used to save up to get our own quarter, we'd get 3 to 4 quarters. Eat candy! For years and years and years. The ladies. They couldn't play. They were too old. But we got them cottage cheese and milk, we got candy, and we ate a *lot* of candy!

The Lathrop Homes were built for World War II veterans. The women in the projects, the old white women, they would tell us they were waiting for their husbands to come back.

But my father sat us down, my mother sat us down. And they told us that the ladies were waiting for something that was not gonna happen. They were senile. Their husbands had all died in the war. A long time ago.

The ladies would sit outside on the benches all over the projects. We had 300 benches all around the projects. The projects were beautiful. They were gorgeous.

After a while, they finally let the Latinos in there.

First time we hooked up with Latino kids, they came and they started talking Spanish. And we didn't know about Spanish! All we knew was English! And the first time they started talking Spanish we just tripped out. Oh my God, it was a foreign country! We were like, "How do you do your mouth like that?" They talk Spanish so fast. And we never heard this kind of language, so that freaked us out.

So we got to know 'em——they were young, they were kids like us. There was like three or four families. They were Mexicans and Puerto Ricans that they put in first. And we were just getting used to them.

And then they wanted us to come to their house and eat rice and beans.

Well we laughed at them. We thought it was a joke. We thought it was regular beans. Pork and beans. It wasn't. It was Puerto Rican rice and beans. The beans were black. So we thought they had burned them up.

But when we took that first spoonful and put it in our mouths, our mouths just shattered.

Danny smiles at the memory of something that tasted that good.

It was *so good*! And then we started eating their food and it was all delicious. They had the best food! And that's how we started knowing them. From when we were eating with them. Then we started knowing their words, their language.

Then came the Chinese. The projects started getting mixed. We started eating with them, too. Liking their food.

But things started changing. The old white ladies, they started moving out. A lot of them died. Our rents got really, really cheap.

Then they threw the hillbillies into the projects. They came. So we were like a big old pot. We had beans, corn, Chinese food, everything. We were all trying to get to know each other. Mixing the pot. And that was how it started.

It all started with the food.

Then they threw in some Indians. They had long hair. Then after a while, they threw in more blacks. Now it was really mixed. The neighborhood changed again.

It was like a family. Our project was small. So everybody stuck together. We were like a family. At Lathrop Homes, there's 950 apartments. I've been to every single one of them. I've been on every roof. I've been in every basement. My father was the head janitor. Not right away. He turned into the head janitor. But that's another story. In the early times, he didn't have a job. So he pulled garbage, got pieces of steel and metal to the dump. Scrap metal. That's how we lived. That's how we paid bills. But then my father turned into the head janitor.

My Mother was the head of the PTA. She was the head of every agency they had in the area. She was the head of the Boys Club. The Boys Club was in the basement. My mother headed up the Boys Club. Because we had no place to play.

When we started growing up, we went to Schneider School. That's the only school around. They had other schools. But we went to Schneider.

Now we lived right down the street from Riverview Amusement Park. You remember Riverview? Riverview was our playground. We had the biggest playground in the city of Chicago.

Since we were poor, they gave us free tickets every day. Every day! Thousands of tickets they gave us. Stacks. Riverview was so big that they had 103 rides going all at once.

I remember the Hells Angels hung out there a lot. The motorcycle gang. They were there. They'd have fights. We used to sneak out and watch. They had chains. Motorcycle jackets. They were wild.

One day we're at Riverview. We're watching the boat ride. We're throwing rocks in the water. And all of a sudden the security guards, no, they were the cops, they came and they snatched us. "C'mon! You hurt this lady!'"

I said, we ain't hurt no lady! We know what we're doing. We don't do that stuff.

So they took us over and sure enough there was this lady. Blood was pouring out of her head. She was hurt bad. And they were gonna put us in the same car as her. And take us wherever they take little kids. Audy Home or something.

So seeing this poor lady hurt like that, I thought about my mother. My Mother was the strictest mother in the world. I was more scared of my mother than jail or death or anything. I mean, my mother—that was it.

So I knew my mother would find out if I was in jail. And I knew that if I went to jail, I'd get beat to death anyway. But I was really more scared as to what my mother would do if she found out I was in jail.

So I took off and started running.

I don't know if you remember a commercial that was on, it was on for Malt-O-Meal. And there was a song, *(sings)*

Get on the Malt-O-Meal mobile.
Get on the Malt-O-Meal mobile.
Puts a spark in your engine!
See how good you feel!

And as I ran I sang that song to myself, psyching myself to keep me running. I take off and all my friends they took off, too. And they chased us all the way back from Riverview, all the way to the projects.

And we all hid. We all ran home. Changed clothes. And we all went out again. And they looked for us. Because this lady was seriously hurt. Her head was busted wide open. So they looked for us. But they couldn't figure out who we were.

I never knew who hurt that lady because people came from all over to Riverview. From the South Side, from the West Side. So I didn't know who it was.

Riverview was there for years. And then the owner—he got tired of being sued. We watched, we were there when the guy fell from the Bob Sled. We were all there. Thousands of people saw this. Guy on the ride stood up, waves to his wife, he hit the sign, big sign that says BOB and he fell all the way down the wood thing. Killed him. That was the end of Riverview.

It was like Coney Island in New York. All the old rides, the Castle, the Sutton Castle, I was so scared of that, my brother got me so scared of that. He said, you fall in there, we can't get you out!

I was yelling, screaming, didn't want to go back there again. And the parachute?

Remember the parachute?

Riverview was gone. So our neighborhood changed again.

The Lathrop Homes in the 1960s:
The River and the Gangs

But I knew our neighborhood. I knew the projects. They could close down the projects right now. They could put cops everywhere. But I bet you I could get in there.

The river runs right by the projects. The Chicago River. Runs all the way downtown. And things happen in the river, by the river.

People die in the river.

Friend of mine, a girl, she was doing drugs, she jumped in the river and killed herself.

I was talking to her an hour or so before she did it.

I swam in that river, I fell in that river. And the bridge. The old Diversey Bridge. Oh my God there are more stories about that bridge. That whole bridge would shake. Solid wood. But when a bus comes the whole thing shakes like jelly so you hang on for dear life. Under the bridge we had a rope. We used to swing across. One day my friend pushed me in and the bloodsuckers, the leeches, got me. I had leeches all over me. And you gotta burn 'em off.

Every year the circus used to come to town and dump the elephant waste in the river. Big huge balls of elephant waste, and we used to play with those.

The deepest part of the river is 40 feet.

While we were playing in that river, in the 60s, the gangs started coming in. We had a gang called the Deuces. My gang. The Insane Deuces. It wasn't serious at the get go. At the beginning. But it got serious.

I had four branches. I had Leavitt Deuces, Clybourn Deuces, Damen, and Logan Square. I ran it all. Over 200 guys. But I was smart. I knew how to run it. I didn't publicize myself. I stayed in the shadows.

We ran all the gangs out of there that threatened us. We went to the school called Schurz. And they didn't like us coming to their school because we were a mixed gang. We were black, white, Chinese, everybody. We were mixed. And they were just white gangs. They were tough.

We had colors. Our colors were green and black. But the main gang, the one we always used to fight was the Royals. We almost destroyed them. In fact I think we did. I was around 17, 18 years old.

The power. You never been in a gang and you never been a leader. So you don't know how much power that is. You got power over life and death. All you gotta say is, "Get 'em."

The dues they give you, anything you order, they get you.

The power I had is like being the President of the United States. It's fantastic. The dictators—I know how that feels. To have that power. It's unbelievable. It's a burden, but it's everything. I had a little bit of power and it was fantastic.

That was a time when lots was going on. Like President Kennedy. Kennedy was the black man's king. Without Kennedy, we wouldn't have had a lot of stuff. When he was shot, I heard it at school. The President died.

It was a big thing. But not too big. Until we started getting into it. And the shock hit us. Then all the teachers started crying. And it was like . . . why all these white teachers crying?

And then I came home and my Mother was crying. And it was freaking me out. And I said, "Mama why you cryin'?" And she said to me "That white guy was everything! He's the one gave us our rights! Without him, we wouldn't have had what we have! He was the best President in the world. Don't you ever forget that. You got to understand that!"

And I watched and I listened and that's when it hit me. And I wanted to know *more* about him. 'Cause I was a kid. I didn't know. So I wanted to know more. He must have really been the man. And I saw other people crying and they were black and they were crying over this white president and I was like . . . man! He was a white guy and I didn't know he did so much for us. And our neighborhood was sad, the whole of Chicago was sad. We all watched the burial, we saw his little kid saluting. His son.

Then Martin Luther King started coming. And I knew about Martin Luther King.

And when King got killed they started rioting. Me and my friends, we rioted. But we was on the North Side. And that was nothing. We were acting out.

Like pretend rioting.

On the West Side, the South Side, they were robbing stores, burning them down. We were nothing like that. We were knocking over wooden crates and shooting blanks from guns. We wasn't that bad.

Then came Kennedy's brother. Another good Kennedy. He's gonna get it.

He got shot down, too.

And that's when my mother got cancer.

Project Pride

I didn't know cancer; I didn't know what that meant, how bad that was. And then the doctor . . . he tricked me. That son of a bitch. He tricked me. He tricked the shit out of me. He said my mother's gonna be all right.

He said, "We're gonna find a cure for cancer in ten years." And then my mother, it was breast cancer. They cut off her breast. She lost all her friends because they didn't want to be around her. It was an ugly scar. And her best friend just stopped seeing her. And my mother went downhill from there. *(voice soft)* That was the tragedy in our lives. When my mother was dying. And she suffered two and a half years. There was a lot of pain. And I have . . . I have regrets . . . 'cause I shoulda helped her more. I shoulda helped her more. And like, your parents, your parents are everything. I didn't realize that. I was young. I regret it to this day.

And then when my father got sick, I helped him out. Because I didn't want to have those same regrets.

But my mother, my mother was so smart. She knew how to deal with big corporations. I don't know if you've ever heard of a company, it was called Stewart Warner. They made airplane parts. They had a plant. It was huge. Right in the neighborhood. And my mother, she went there and talked to the men that ran that company and got the money to start up the Boys Club in the basement of our project.

She talked to the actor Danny Thomas. He helped with the money. With the donations. That all came because of my mother.

My mother was ahead of her time. She organized the whole thing, the Boys Club. It was in one basement and that got too crowded, so she got another basement. Then that got too crowded, so my mother figured out how to get a whole building built.

After my Mom—bad times.

My father took over. People tried to trick my father, take his money.

Nobody wanted me. As she was dying, my mother was worried about me. She said to my father, "Make sure somebody takes care of Danny."

My mother was a leader in the community. My father was a survivor.

So I got traits of both of them. That's how I made it.

'Bout that time they started killing gang leaders. I started backing out. It took years. Other gangs started hitting my areas.

Cops made me move. The gang thing—they started killing all my boys. I got out of there. Stopped representing. Hanging around. My boys got killed, they moved away, they went to jail. Gangs got smaller. I was 27, 28 before I got out.

You ever been to the project? Lathrop? You ever been there? You have to go over there! We have to go there and check it out! That could be part of your book! I could show you around! I could show you the whole thing. Man, you would know what I'm talking about. Cause they might tear it down. And Lathrop been there since the 1930s. Take some pictures. There's a lot of vacant apartments. The Boys Club, cause of my mother, then there's the Church of the Good News, my mother helped build that too. It's on the corner.

I love Lathrop.

I'll be there till the day I die. I don't care; I'm halfway around the world. I'll always come back to Lathrop.

Once you're from the projects, the projects stay with you. The projects make you proud. I'm from the projects. It makes you strong. Project people don't turn around. Project people don't back down. Project people help people. We help poor people. People say "Hey man, you gotta dime? You gotta nickel?" You say, "Yeah, I got it. Here you go." I don't have no job. But I got 50 cents in my pocket. Here you go. Here's a dime. I got five bucks in my pocket? Here, you take a dollar.

Today

I hustle. On Thursdays. I got a corner. That's my spot. I panhandle. But I make people feel good. I see people, I say, "How you doing sir? How you doing ma'am? You havin' a nice day? Maybe help

24

me out with a little change? If you can't that's okay. But don't look so down!'"

And they say to me, "'Hey thanks for saying that to me. I needed that. That does make me feel good." Like this place here. The Pantry. The Pantry gives you serious help. Because we are talking about food here. That's serious.

The Pantry and the good food the church serves up Wednesday night. It makes people feel good.

How long I been coming here? I don't know. Long time.

What's it like when you come here? What do you do?

I try to relax people. Lady walks by, I say, "'Hey, don't look so sad. Things gonna be better. Maybe not today. But they will get better." Some of 'em don't respond. But some of 'em come back.

I need it, and I know they got it. I'll take a dollar. A dime. A penny. But give me something. And if you give me nothing, I love you anyway. Maybe next time.

Like I said, my mother was a leader. My father was a survivor. I got traits from both of them.

Now? I'm staying in Humboldt Park. I pay rent. I get SSI and I go to school. Part of Truman College. Getting my GED. But that's another story.

That's another chapter.

Chapter One is Lathrop.

CHERYL
Question Mark

———

Sitting across the table from Cheryl, a black-haired, bright-eyed woman in her 30s, you can still see that hint of mischievous fun that made musicians across the club scene in Chicago say, "Oh, you're a music journalist? Sure! You can interview me. And right now would be fine."

She's interviewed hundreds of musicians. But no one has ever interviewed her. When asked for a title to her story, she answers, "Title it 'Question Mark.'"

Like almost every other client, Cheryl heard about the Common Pantry from a friend.

Her friend is with her today. This is Cheryl's first visit. While Cheryl tells her story, the friend plays with Cheryl's three-year-old daughter, a squealing, curious bundle of bright-eyed energy running

*around the tables of the Common Pantry, making
people smile wherever she runs.*

———

I get told that I'm a worthless piece of crap. I get that a lot.

My parents aren't real happy with me. Every time I go see them, I get to hear what a big disappointment I am.

I have a brother. He has a lot of money. Two homes. And I hear, "You should be like that! You should be like your brother or your sister!" My boyfriend tells me the same thing.

I don't have a job and I don't work. And I never talk about me. Even when I had a job. Even when I was working 12-hour shifts, I never talked about me.

So, it feels good to tell my story. I see a lot of positives. I *never* get to talk about me. No one ever wants to hear about me. Not in any kind of objective sense, where there's no judgment, no advice, no warnings. Talking like this? When I can just talk? This makes me think that I really am somebody.

My early years?

I was raised Catholic. The education was excellent. I paid attention. I was that girl in the front row. You know the one: answered all the questions; paid attention!

My childhood was relatively good. I was adopted. My parents sacrificed. I went to a private school. I was good at science and history and journalism. I went to college. Ended up doing court reporting, and then medical transcription. The medical terms weren't hard for me. And I'm a good proofreader. I took the test for medical transcription. Took the test., got 100%. I did that for six years. I liked it.

(She brightens as she speaks of accomplishments—and as her story unfolds, there are many.)

I got married pretty early. Then I got divorced and thought—what am I going to do now? So I went to school to become a nurse. Graduated as an LPN [licensed practical nurse].

There's a shortage of those. Lots of jobs. But I can't do that anymore.

Why not?

That's a whole different story. Here's what happened.

I had an injury. Hurt my back. Got a herniated disk. And I got hooked on painkillers. Started on Percocet, then I'd go in to the clinic near where I live. They'd give me injections. Sometimes morphine. I had to work, so the doctor gave me whatever I wanted. Then it just grew.

That went on for about eight years, till I finally couldn't take it anymore and I took myself off. I could have had the stuff as long as I wanted. But I knew it was hurting me. So I took myself off, went into a methadone program.

I kicked it. I've seen psychiatrists and all that. But I kicked it myself. I stayed clean.

But I can't go back to being a nurse because I'd be the one in charge of the drugs. And I can't do that. I'd always be the charge nurse. That's just the way it would happen. I have a lot of experience. These days LPNs are charge nurses a lot. And I've done dialysis. I've done a lot. Everywhere I ever worked as a nurse, they always made me charge nurse. I really am pretty good at it, which is fine unless you're addicted and in charge of the drugs.

And I just know I can't trust myself with that. The only way for me to stay clean is to stay away. And I have a daughter now. I got pregnant and I have my daughter now. And it's just us. So, I have to stay clean.

I mean I still don't feel right. But I'm clean.

I do have really bad anxiety. It's hard for me to talk to people. I always feel like I'm bothering people.

And I used to be a journalist. I'd do concert reviews for a lot of music magazines. My stuff was out there; I had a lot of work. All the music clubs and CD reviews. I worked a lot. I knew that scene.

In the music world there weren't a lot of women, at least not back in the 1990s. So I always got in. It was easy for me. Everybody would talk to a woman. *(Laughs.)* And I didn't look like I do now.

I never had a hard interview. I looked the part. I was the only woman, so I got a lot of attention. I had them calling me. I'd be talking to one guy and another would be like, "When are you gonna interview me? Can we make an appointment?"

When I get down now, it makes me feel better to think of those days. I took photos of every single interview I ever did. But that book, the one where I kept them all, a girl who was jealous of me stole it. So the book is gone.

I still like that music. I made some money. I traveled a lot: Sweden; England; everywhere in the United States.

But I drifted out of the scene. I got depressed. It was like I was some sort of human knot. Everything I did to try and untie it just made it tighter.

Now, I don't have any real social outlet. I met my boyfriend at the clubs at the end of my journalism time. Interviewing people was the thing that got me able to talk to people. Otherwise I'd be just too shy. So with the interviewing gone, I don't really talk with people all that much.

Honestly? I don't how we make it. I don't know what we'd do without the Pantry. In fact, even with the Common Pantry, I've had to start to hustle to get money.

Tell me about the hustle.

I'll go by a big "L" station. I'll have my child with me. And I'll say, "Can you spare a couple of dollars? I have to get on the train."

It's really embarrassing. *(Laughs.)* And the really funny part is that everything I'm saying when I'm hustling is true! I really *don't* take drugs. I really *don't* have any money! It's really embarrassing. It's sad.

I'm trying to get aid, but I keep getting turned down. Because they see what I am, all that I've done, the education I have, the fact that I'm a nurse and they go, "Pfft, what's the problem?"

Oh, I know there are places where I could be a nurse where there are no drugs, but I haven't found them. And one of the things about all the education, I don't know if it's good or bad, but you do know what's wrong. I'm clinically depressed. I'm in a study at Loyola right now. I signed myself up for it.

I don't really relax. My daughter is three. And she's a handful. My older children, the kids I had back at the beginning in my 20s, were always with relatives because I was always working. I worked a lot. I'd come home, and they would be sleeping. So this is the first one I get to see really growing up. It's stressful.

Right now I'm staying with my boyfriend. He's in the area. He's really sick right now. He can't work anymore. So now neither of us is working, and it's tough times.

I want to go into medical billing and coding. It's easy. I could do it at home. I could do it anywhere. I like data entry. I need to go to school for that. And I don't have any money.

Most of all? I want my daughter to do what she wants to do, not what somebody else tells her to do, what somebody else tells her is right. Because that's the way it always was for me.

If I had done what I wanted to do? It would have been totally different!

I would have gotten a scholarship to get me into college, journalism, or been an English teacher.

What writer would you teach if you were an English teacher?

Louisa May Alcott. I really liked her. She wrote so many interesting things, different genres. She had a lover that was 22 when she was 37.

I go to the library a lot. I can read a book in a couple of hours. Maybe I would have been a librarian. My daughter, she loves to read. She'll get her book, and just sit down and go.

Like I said, if I was able to make the decisions? It would have been different.

But I can't give up, for my daughter. She's what keeps me going. It's just me. Her father isn't around. So it's just me to be an example. That's what keeps me going.

So, yeah, it really does feel good to tell my story. I see a lot of positives. I *never* get to talk about me.

(She smiles. Suddenly she's 10 years younger.) Yes, I've thought of writing again, writing my story. People have even said to me, "You should write about all your experiences."

What would I call it? That's a good question. When I wrote, I'd never start writing till I had my title. At that time, a lot of the writing was just "I'm gonna start writing!" But I always had a title.

What should you call the chapter on me? I don't know.

Call it "Question Mark."

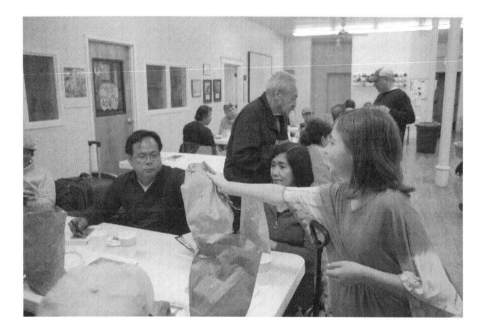

ERNIE
A Work in Progress

———

If homelessness were a university, then Ernie would be a professor. Not a science or math professor— because there is nothing logical in the way his story flows. Ernie, with his scraggly white beard and battered baseball cap, would teach philosophy or the arts, something where the answers need not always be complete. His story is told in vivid images and strings of emotional pearls.

Great gaps in memory are created by his years on the streets. He leaves out large pieces of the puzzle, inviting the listener to figure out what's between the lines of the story. He jumps from freight trains rolling into Corpus Christi at age 20, then back to childhood abuse. He and his sister hiding under the bed when he was 8; and then he leaps to the worries of the future and a grandson. He is sad but realistic about the cycle of poverty continuing across generations.

Soft-spoken and polite, he is often apologetic and timid. The strength of his survival skills is subtle and understated. Ernie reminds the listener, just by the way he is, that no one ever knows somebody else's complete story.

Even if one listens hard, very hard, one won't hear or know everything. But what one will hear are the important parts. And maybe that's enough.

———

I'm a work in progress. Just like you. Just like all of us. I'm a work in progress.

Tell me about your parents.

My mother only gave me what she was taught. My Mother gave me brutality.

It wasn't her fault. My mother, she was raised hard-core Indian: Yakama *(a tribe of the slopes of the Cascade Mountains in Washington State)*. She gave me what she knew. She didn't go to training school to be a parent.

In a sense, knowing what I know today, it was better off not being with her, my mother. I might have died if I had stayed with her.

So what was it like for you when you were young?

I was running away all the time. I always did that. I ran away. The police were finding me underneath the house, hiding, always hiding in places like that.

What about your father?

My father was a field worker. He came from the Philippines. He worked the fields: lettuce, romaine, carrots, cabbage. He traveled. To me, I didn't see nothing bad about him. But he didn't give me no love, no teaching. He was too busy. There was no bond between him and my mother. She was a wild Indian.

I seen certain things that transpired in her fighting. I seen knives. Me and my sister, we'd hide beneath the bed. When the knives came out, we'd hide. Or I'd run away.

My mother was always fighting. So I didn't see my father all that much. He didn't come to stay with us all that often.

What memories are the strongest?

There is so much to remember. But I forget a lot of things, too. I remember one time we stayed in a camp, a place for workers, like a worker's state. And I guess we had our own place at the camp, all the workers, living together.

My mother took us all over California. There wasn't any one place that was home.

Where were you born?

I was born in Salinas, California., on the Monterey Peninsula. But I can't remember a time when we weren't moving.

What about school?

I went to a Catholic school for a brief period. Catechism, I went to that. But I didn't have no real religious training as a child.

I *think* I had an experience back then . . . I don't remember. But I think I had an experience. I met a Bible-believing person. Not a Catholic. And his hand, if I believe this, his hand changed my life. He put his hand on me and it changed my life. I didn't understand that until years, years, years later. I didn't know about the Holy Spirit then. But I do have the memory of that hand on me.

> *He pauses. Goes quiet. What else do you remember about that holy person?*

The person that placed his hand on me, I don't know what he did. But I just remember for a fact that when an individual loves Jesus Christ, when he touches you, praying for you, laying his hands on you, then miracles happen.

> *So this was around the time when you were a teenager. What was it like for you as a teenager?*

My teenager time was in reform schools. Where I grew up really was in reform schools. Started when I was I was somewhere around 11 or 12, always running away. When the judge asked me if I wanted to go back home, I told him no, no more abuse. So they sent me to reform school.

My sisters were lucky. They were fortunate. They didn't have to endure what I endured.

> *In thinking back to what he had to endure, Ernie begins to free associate: a thread from childhood; a story unconnected to anything he's said so far, but perhaps a clue.*

Why was I talking to the judge? My sister, she told me to go to the mailbox. To open the letters and see if there was money inside. I just wasn't that smart. I believe it was my sister.

You did what your sister told you to do? You believed her? And sometimes that did not work out? Maybe you took some blame?

I believed it because she did things like pissing in the damn bottle, give it to me, and tell me it was soda pop.

So they came and got me, and that's why I was talking to the judge. They got me and not my sister. The court decided to send me to reform school. My life changed. I became what they called "under protection."

Reform school, it's like torture. Like gladiators fighting all the time. They give those places nice names, but you have to fight a lot.

You got a lot of people who go in there, who go into reform schools, and they all got problems. Some worse than others, but they all got problems. And you live among people who have problems, and if you were like me, if you were Indian, you had to fight a lot.

Looking back through the years, I wonder why I was in reform school. I was locked up and I was tortured and I didn't have an easy time. But I never told my sister that. I never told her. My sister was lucky. She didn't have to endure what I endured.

There have been times I wanted to tell her, tell my sister all about what happened to me. Because they should have sent me to a foster home, not to an institution; to a home where you have another person.

I got out when I was, oh, 18 I guess. But I had to stay in California because I was on parole until I was 21. Then I took off.

You were on parole for . . .?

For being trouble.

So you left California as soon as you were off parole?

I hitchhiked, caught a freight. And I ended up in Corpus Christi, Texas. Just after Hurricane Celia hit. *(Note: Hurricane Celia hit Corpus Christi Texas on August 3, 1970, killing 15 people and causing damage equivalent of $2.6 billion in today's dollars.)*

After that my life started changing. There was this place where they helped homeless people, taught you the Bible. If you were hungry, they fed you. And I was hungry. I didn't even know if I wanted to live anymore.

Then I had an experience with Jesus Christ. I started learning the Word of God. God intervened in my life and he started teaching me about man, about how to read the Bible, and

I started reading the Bible. There is healing in the Bible. There is past, present and future. I own a Bible now. Haven't read it in a while, but I read literature that is connected to the Bible, that comes from the Bible. I read stories.

After Corpus Christi, I was searching, still searching. Then it was El Paso, Texas. I got married in Texas, and I left her. I married a woman who had children, but I kept moving.

When I left Texas, I hitchhiked to different places, Louisiana, Georgia. And I ended up in Birmingham, Alabama. And then somewhere along the line, I was homeless.

What brought me to Chicago? My sister was living here. I came to visit her. She was working for the airlines, flying. My sister said to me, "Come to Chicago, my husband will teach you a trade. He'll teach you how to paint."

That was a mistake. Coming to Chicago was a mistake. I should have stayed in Alabama. I could have learned plumbing. I had met this other girl. Her father was a plumber. He would have taught me. But I was offered a place to stay in Chicago, a chance to not be homeless.

My sister's husband treated me like a slave. I had to babysit their kids. They made me a slave. I lived with them. They were using me. Paying me less than everyone else. So I eventually got out. I became homeless here.

What happened to my sister? My sister got transferred to Texas. I talk to her once in a great while. I wished her Happy Birthday.

What about work in Chicago?

I was working for a while. The woman I was married to before in Texas, she came here to Chicago. She was pregnant when I met her. Gave the child my name. There were more children now. We had children together. She wanted my help to take care of the children.

So I took care of the children. I was having problems with finances and trying to teach a child not to wet the bed. But I got all the kids enrolled in school, a good school. Then one of the children got hurt in school. He broke the femur in his leg.

That must have been hard. What happened after he broke his leg?

They said I broke the leg. They said I did it. They tried everything to destroy me. Brought me to the police station. But they couldn't keep me because there was nothing. There was no proof. DCFS was called. They came and took away all my children.

This was a while back. Are you in contact with your children now?

Within the last few months, my children, the oldest and the youngest, too, they got in contact. It is God's blessing.

I got tears in my eyes right now. I've probably talked like this, told all of this, less than a handful of times. No one's ever asked me to tell my story before. And as I talk right now, I'm praising God because I know I need his help. And God says to me, you lift me up; I'll lift you up. So it's a blessing to talk.

I know I'm sick. I don't know how much time I have left in this world. I don't know how much time is left for mankind. Medical help? I lost my medicine. Hard to hold on to stuff on the street.

But I've been blessed here, blessed by this place, the Common Pantry, the Church, the Wednesday Welcome Meal. I've been blessed by this place.

I come here for the Wednesday meal, for the food. But I came to play cards first.

I been blessed to come out of the cold, play cards, get out of the streets. I don't go to libraries 'cause I have a tendency to fall asleep. So I come here. I have associates here, here and on the streets. I wouldn't call them friends. I really don't have friends. I have associates. The people I play cards with, they're associates. I like this place 'cause it's safe.

See, this is a place.

And on the street, you don't have a place. Not a place where it's safe. In the winter, like now, that's when it's really hard to find a place. And I don't have a place. Haven't had a place since I was married. I lost that place. I goofed up. I been homeless this time, oh, around five years. I sleep anyplace, out by the lake, police stations, anyplace.

What's next for you?

What's next? Thanks to this place *(Common Pantry)* and another place, I'm gonna have my own apartment soon. We'll see how that goes. That lady, Kelly, she's helped me. Once in a while I get food from the pantry. I took some food to this person's house. Asked them to cook for me. This time if I get food I can put it in the refrigerator at my new apartment.

> *Everything you've been through, do you think you'd be in a position to help other people going through what you've been through? Ernie thinks for a moment and thoughtfully nods his head yes.*

I know the power of God. I used to try and evangelize. God is still working with me. I am still being shaped. I am a work in progress.

And as Ernie says that last line, a cell phone rings.

****

Postscript: Ernie did get his apartment, thanks to the folks at Thresholds. Furnished with donations for Epiphany Church members and Common Pantry volunteers, Ernie received a bed, a microwave, a shower curtain, pots and pans —the basics to help him get back on his feet. And a shopping trip to Jewel with Epiphany members helped stock his cupboards.

But change is never easy. As is true for all of us "works in progress," what we know always holds a certain comfort that is absent from the unknown. So the first couple weeks found Ernie back on the streets with his "associates," every few nights or so, his new apartment remaining vacant. But that's fading. He's now sleeping in his apartment every night. He's got cell phone numbers of Common Pantry volunteers and he uses them. He called the other day and asked for prayers for his daughter and grandson, now living temporarily in a homeless shelter; prayers to help break the cycle that can move on through the generations, if the stories, if the communication, if the caring stops.

Prayers for a restful night in his safe warm bed.

At home.

ANGELINA
Gems

———

Angelina carries herself like a silent princess. She has perfect posture. She doesn't walk, she flows. She makes an observer imagine Aztec royalty.

Walking to the interview room, she leads the way, moving away from the bustle and noise of the Fellowship Hall, where the Common Pantry clients congregate while playing cards, talking, reading magazines, and working with Kelly and Matty to help solve the challenges of everyday life.

Once inside the room where we will talk, Angelina simply looks at her two children, a pre-teen boy and a younger girl. They smile shyly, and sit down at the table. The girl begins to diligently color. The young boy sits with the patience of an old soul. The children are fluent in both English and Spanish. Angelina speaks halting English. So she tells her story in Spanish with the help of the translator.

The quiet dignity of the small family fills the little room before a word is spoken.

———

The Pantry helps a lot because of the crisis, the financial situation in the country. There are no jobs, no money. I keep up. I listen to the news, read the news.

As she speaks through the translator, her two children say nothing. They are planted in their chairs, like small living lessons in patience and grace.

I live near Kedzie and Belmont. This is my neighborhood. It's okay. Yes, I know it's okay. I've been in Chicago 11 years. Originally, I come from Mexico.

I come to the Common Pantry because a friend of mine told me about it. I've been coming a year.

I have the Link card (a "food stamps" electronic card) and the Common Pantry. This is what we have for our family. I use it all.

Even in translation, the serene tones of her simple statements come through.

I like cooking; saving money, making my own meals at home. Compared to other people that I know, I know that I'm special because of that. There are smiles when I cook.

Tell me about the differences between Chicago and Mexico.

In Mexico it is quieter. We had a house. I did not have to pay bills or pay rent. Here there is stress. But my husband was here, so we came to reunite the family. My husband is in construction. He was without a job for three to four months. She smiles, as does the older boy. Then three weeks ago he got a job again. In construction!

Tell me about religion in your life.

I am a Catholic. I go to my church all the time.

She stops with that as if there is simply nothing else to say on that subject.
Let's talk about work.

For work, for money, I try to help my husband. I make bead jewelry.

She pulls out a small plastic bag of bright, multi-colored beads, and then points at the bracelets on her wrist.

I buy the beads. Make the jewelry. I sell it to family and friends, my jewelry.

The most important thing to know about me? I know how to keep a trust. I am a listener. People tell me things.

I like to help people. The family of my husband lost their house, and I helped. Moral . . . spiritual . . . I listen to them. I have a personality that helps people. Yes, people want to talk to me.

The translator chimes in: "Every time she is here, she is looking for something to do with her kids. Her kids are always busy, never wild. They are different than all the other kids. Every year at Christmas the church selects three families for presents. Last year it was this family. It's for these kids. They are quiet; never running around getting into things; well educated. Such amazing children."

I want the best for my kids: go to college, study, have a career. A better future for my kids than it is right now for my husband and I.

She turns to the young man.

What will you study?

He answers in the clear, engaged tones of an exceptionally bright young man who would be the shining-eyed, true pride of any parent, anywhere.

"First, graphic design. A graphic designer. I like drawing. I like technology. Game development or the technology of special effects in film production."

I ask him if sometimes he helps his Mother translate. He politely nods and says,

"Sometimes."

I ask him if he's heard of Flashpoint Academy, a relatively new school located downtown specializing in his interests. His eyes light up. As we all get up and open the door back into the noise of a filled up Fellowship Hall— clients waiting for their number to be called for grocery distribution—the young boy asks,

"This is just downtown? Here in Chicago?"

I tell him yes. He nods. And in that nod comes the feeling that he won't forget this small piece of information. The young man listens.

Now I'll be looking for you to be famous! I'll remember you!

The young boy beams. This is a young man, one can't help think, who will do what he sets his mind to do, and who will add something important to the world.

Angelina and her daughter stand at his side, quietly proud.

WAYNE
An American Spirit

You can see it in Wayne's face. You know it when he starts talking. Two themes dominate his life: pain and rebirth; a life of devastating hardship, then constantly starting over.

A large physical presence in his 40s, Wayne's long dark black hair and deep blue eyes capture you as you listen to his quiet, slow cadence. An occasional tremor ripples through his left arm. His wears a constant weary smile, the kind of smile that comes to push back the pain.

At age 13, his solo hitchhiking journey spanned the entire country. He now lives in a room at the YMCA down the street from Common Pantry. He tells his story in the measured yet passionate, knowing tones of an ancient and spiritual soul.

Life was kinda good until I hit about seven. Then my father got shot and passed.

Blackfoot Indian and Italian: I guess that is a pretty unusual combination. We, my family, we were different.

My father was the Italian. My father was a police officer. He was a lieutenant in Boston riot control. He was pure Italian. What he said went; head of the house; king of the castle.

I was a little mischief-maker. I remember one time; he was having dinner for six people. He had bought lobsters. I wanted to help him. So I decided to clean the lobsters. With a bubble bath. Got 'em all in the tub, poured in the bubble path. Soaped them all up.

I just wanted to help him.

After he passed, and I had no father, a lot of police officers were always coming by the house, taking me places, watching me grow, helping me become a man.

But my dad was gone.

My earliest memory? Earliest memory is when we got the dog. He was a German shepherd, purebred. His name was Dusty. I loved that dog to death. That dog loved me. That dog and me clicked better than me and my father.

One time I was gonna get a whippin', I don't remember why, but Dusty wouldn't let my dad do it. Dusty spoke to him. Wouldn't let him hit the boy. I loved my dog. When my father passed, they gave me the dog. It helped.

He was my big brother with a tail. This was back when dogs were allowed to go into the grocery stores. So Dusty always went with me. Even in grocery stores. We were like Siamese twins. Dusty protected me.

Then after my dad died, I kinda rebelled. I became a troublemaker.

Somebody took my father. I got mad.

I was getting Dusty to be mad with me because he could sense my mood. My mom tried to discipline me, but there was no way she could do it with the dog. Dog slept by me, ate with me. We clicked like two peas in a pod. Only thing different about us was that he had fur.

From 7 to 11, life went on. I was getting in trouble now and then. You test your parents. So I tested my mom; nothing with the police, little things.

When I turned 11, my mom passed away. I found her dead in bed. That's when things really started to go bad.

Now I was mad at the world. First my dad, then my mom. Why is God doing this to me? Doesn't he like me?

I understood my dad's job. I knew why he died. But my mom, that I didn't understand. I didn't know my Mom had real bad health problems.

It happened like this. One day I came home from school for lunch, and my lunch wasn't made. And me being half Italian and half Indian, I was like, all yelling and mad, "My food's not on the table? What's going on?"

Dusty was acting strange that day, too. My mom was in bed. I touched her and she didn't wake up. So I went to the upstairs neighbor and I told her, "Mom's acting really strange. She's not waking up, she's not making my lunch." The woman upstairs made me lunch. She said, "Your mom is just sleeping. Why don't you eat lunch and just go back to school?"

I knew something was bad because of the way Dusty was acting: pacing, like a nervous person would do in a hospital.

When I got home from school, my aunt was there. She tried to tell me what was going on. She told me mom had gone to heaven. I said, so mom is going with dad? She said, "Exactly."

And I said, "well if my Mom and Dad are in heaven, why can't I go?"

She said to me, "God doesn't want you to go yet. God wants you to live with me."

My aunt was a very stern woman. There was an uncle, too, very stern. Do what you're told. They were Italian.

I was with them for two years. I hated, despised them. They took my father's pension money. They bought me clothes but they could have put some of it away. Bought a savings bond or something. They had two kids. So I was the odd man out.

They weren't at all like my Mom. Not at all.

My Mom was a Blackfoot Indian.

I believe in Indian culture. I believe strongly in Italian culture. I can see more than a person who only has one culture.

I am stern with myself.

But I'm more focused on my Indian background. The Indians had a rough time as they went through history. I believe in that. When I pass, I'll be taken and disposed of on a reservation. I've been to a reservation in Arizona. I've been to reservations in Utah and Arizona. Utah is the most beautiful place I've ever seen. Miles of God's country. Nothing is man-made. I respect that, nature. I used to climb, rock climb, repel. God's country. There are no commercial buildings anywhere. Most beautiful, wide-open, cleanest, clearest place I've ever seen.

How did I see all that? How did I get out?

I left. One day I just got up and left. I was 13 years old and very stern. I was like a 30-year-old man.

First my dad had died. Then my mom. Then Dusty. Dusty was with me till I was 12. When he died, I had no one.

I packed a little bag and hitchhiked across the country, from Lynn, Massachusetts, to San Diego. It was as far as I could imagine.

I was picked up by a reverend. Right outside of Lynn. He says, "Where's your parents?" I said, "I don't want to talk about that, I'm going to California. You want to give me a ride?" I was very stern with the man.

He kind of chuckled and asked me if I knew what a reverend is. I said, "Yeah, I know what a reverend is, I know what a pastor is, I know what a preacher is."

We drove straight across the whole country together. He took me to a youth hostel in East L.A., a Christian-based youth hostel, a house of misfits.

That's when the gang affiliation started. This was about 1973. So there were the two gangs: Bloods and Crips. I didn't join the Crips. I was affiliated. I was what you call a "Neutron." That meant I was hanging with the Crips, being watched by the Crips, protected by the Crips, but not being a member.

I could have gone with the Catholics, gone to the Catholic school. A lady came to talk to me about it. I looked at her like she was crazy. I told her I'd rather be on the streets. I was just about to turn 14 then.

So I met this one Crip. He was the sergeant at arms. He took care of the money and the drugs. He says to me, "You want to make some money?" I said, "How do I do this?"

He told me, "I give you this amount of dope. We put you on a certain corner, you go with the flow." They told me how much money I had to bring back.

So I'd split the bags, make sure I brought their money back to them, keep the rest myself. So everyone was happy, no questions asked.

I had so many people watching me it was funny. But nobody messed with me. I was a white boy in a black neighborhood dealing dope. People figured I was either crazy or that I hadn't got a lick of sense. So nobody bothered me.

Around noon, I'd go into the house, throw down my cash. They wouldn't search me. Why should they search me, I gave them everything they asked for.

I was raking in the money, a white kid selling dope, 14 years old, with three grand in my back pocket.

I was making cake.

I was still living in the youth hostel, but I started thinking I could get an apartment. I was almost 14 now. The gang members were my family, my friends. Why shouldn't they be? I was bringing in three grand a day. I didn't work every day, didn't need to. But I worked most days.

But then somebody at the youth hostel got a social worker to come over and talk to me. I was all on my own, quiet, didn't talk to anybody there. So they sent this social worker.

She knew what I was into. She started telling me I could get killed out there. I told her no big deal. Everybody gets killed anyways.

Death doesn't scare me. Even now, even today, it still doesn't scare me.

She says, "Why don't you go to school? We could put you with this foster family."

I told her I could live with my gang family. First she was nice. But I said no.

She stuck hard. She came on stronger and stronger. She stuck really hard. She'd say to me, "I know what you're doing. I could put you in a sheriff's home."

She was trying to scare me. It was like we were playing chess. I told her I could live with the gang, make money, be protected. Serious money.

Why leave this?

Finally she got me into school. I finally gave her respect because she wouldn't quit, didn't stop. That's how she broke me, broke me and saved me.

I cut down my time dealing dope. Plus, she told me she'd find a place where I could live by myself. She told me that if I stayed in school, she'd fix it so I had this place.

I don't remember her name. I think it was Rita.

She was a good chess player. She was like, "You might be a rook, but I'm a queen."

Crips were cool because I still dealt. Not as much, but I gave them the money they asked for. I was never a member. I was still a neutron, neutral.

In my new place, my apartment, I had to sleep in my tub because of the guns. That way you made sure no bullet ever caught you. But it was my place.

That's where I started getting interested in history, reading, finding out everything I could. I liked history and art. I did charcoal sketches. Now I'm into line art. You draw and figure out the even balance, cut it in quarters. It's about balance. Yeah, it's all about balance. I liked school.

Rita came to see me once a week. She was always there. She stuck with me. Made sure I had food. I was 16 and she was still there. She was determined.

I broke down and finally started calling her Mom because of the way she took care of me. It was a blessing.

I was tired of the big man image and the gang life. Nothing can soothe your soul like Mom can.

I graduated at 16. I went to school in the summers. I figured out if I go in the summers, I could finish quicker. Because I always wanted to go to college. I always stayed a year ahead of myself. Rita was impressed.

I wanted to be a park ranger. I had a thing for nature.

Graduation ceremony came and Rita was there at my graduation. I was totally impressed. I didn't tell her about it, but she was there. She figured it out somehow. I don't know how. But she was there for me. Rita was there.

This is back in the day when people weren't eating up social workers like now.

I was proud of myself because I achieved something by myself. I was a graduate. I felt the spirits of my mom there, the Indian part.

I graduated from high school. And then all hell broke loose.

Suddenly Rita just disappeared.

Rita wasn't there anymore. I think she passed. She must have. She was with me for four years, and then she was gone. Maybe she figured she'd done her time with me, but I think she passed. What am I supposed to think? Rita was gone. She passed. That had to be it.

There I am thinking, looking up in the air, shouting up to God, Why did you take her? Another person looking after me is gone!

So I went back to dealing full time. And this time, I started doing drugs. I had never done it before. So I was splitting packs again, but I wasn't making money. I was a junkie. Four years, it was breaking me. I lost weight. I looked at my face, everything was sucked in. I'm 18, I had to leave.

I looked at a map, put my finger on it. And thought, Miami.

Didn't know a soul.

Packed my clothes and left. It's the only way I could figure out how to leave. Just do it.

And I couldn't have picked a worse place to go. Turns out Miami is about the worst place in the whole United States to be a junkie because coke was cheaper than candy. I go to a bad hotel, hook up with a dealer.

So I had to leave again. Somewhere, somehow, somebody was pushing me out.

I went to Orlando. Found a job in a restaurant, worked my way up to a cook. Got a job working for Disney. Youngest area chef put into a Disney. Went to Disney culinary arts school. Started the job.

My name started getting around as a chef, all these country clubs, people wanted me to come work for them.

I got tired of working for the Mouse (*Disney*). Too many chiefs and not enough Indians. So I got into one of the country clubs. Became an executive chef. Blew their restaurant right to the top. Their profit margin went way up. There I was running a four-star restaurant known for seafood.

So what do I do? I go back to the dope. I had money, so I started making trips to Miami. I was a junkie, so I thought I could handle it, just like any junkie. Coke got the best of me again. I blew my job, quit my job. I was all out of money, about to lose my apartment, so I started going to day labor places. I made 35 bucks a day. This was after making really good money as an executive chef. So I thought, there has got to be something better than day labor.

One day I was looking out the window of my apartment and saw these guys tearing off roofs, and I thought, well I can do that. So I got a job as a roofer. I was making about $120 a day. It was better than the $35 a day for day labor, decent money. Lot harder work, but the money was okay. Did the roofer job for five years.

Got bored one night, went to this biker bar. This sweet little blonde-haired girl came up to me and said, "You have pretty eyes." And that was all it took. We clicked. From the first night we never left each other's side for seven years. They were good years till the end. She was a drinker, and I never drank. I hated drinking.

She's the girl that got me to Chicago. She had family here. Purebred Italian. Her father, he was good. Coming off the plane, I said, I can pick your dad out, little, short Italian guy. So we met. We hit it off. He says, "I love my daughter." I said, "I love your daughter, too." And he says, "You ever hurt my daughter, we're going toe to toe."

I just smiled. I liked the guy a lot.

Then he died.

I really liked the guy.

Then he died, too.

She started drinking, every day. And I was still trying to keep off the coke.

I found a job with a roofing company here in Chicago.

And we finally split up. Great years, up till the end.

I dated another girl about eight months. Got a job managing the building where she lived, handyman work and roofing. If I could have two jobs, I'd take two jobs. I always worked hard. Things were going okay.

Then my arm started shaking. Went to a doctor, three neurologists came in, finally *six* doctors, and they told me I had Parkinson's. I took the "L" home. It hit me. I couldn't work. So I had to tell the roofing company—and they fired me. This was 16 years ago. So I've been living with Parkinson's for 16 years.

Found another roofing company, but I didn't tell them about my health. They did both roofing and wanted to remodel homes. So I went to work for them.

I shook just a little, but I could put that off. I thought I was hiding it pretty well. Things were good. I worked with the Parkinson's for nine years, became a superintendent.

Finally, I told the guys that owned the company, two brothers.

They said, "Wayne, thanks for telling us. We knew something was wrong, but we didn't want to say anything because your job performance is so good." These guys were like my brothers. I would have done anything for these guys.

Then their older brother got laid off from his job. He was a corporate type. So he started working with us all and he started putting into their minds that if I got hurt I'd sue them.

I was the superintendent, everything was fine. We all knew I'd never sue these guys. They were family. So the two brothers said to Mr. Corporate with the bow tie, we want to keep this guy Wayne, so we'll get him a driver and a car so he can check out our jobs. We need him. So they did that, they got me a driver to drive me around. There I was, with a driver and a car!

I read in this medical magazine that pot would stop the shakes. I tried it, and it worked. The brothers were cool, so I showed them.

I worked another four years for them. Parkinson's started getting worse. I was getting —they call it freezing—you walk a few steps freeze and fall.

I knew I couldn't last long. I'd have to get disability.

So, I was working on this lawyer's house, and he said he'd take my case because the two brothers had told him about me. Lawyer said he'd have my disability case approved in a couple of days, I said "Right." I didn't believe it, but then he did it!

I said, "What do I owe you?" He said, "Well, I sent you a bill in the mail." I'm thinking, "Oh no . . ."

I get home, look at the bill and it was a bill for a dollar. He sent me a bill for a dollar. So I knew that I wouldn't have to worry about income.

But without the work, without my brothers who owned the roofing company, I got back into the drugs for a while,

Got bad. Tried to commit suicide. I was in the hospital.

I met this guy Brandon who worked for Metra. He came and saw me at the hospital.

My doctor said I needed brain surgery. He gave me a book on it. I started talking doctor terms to him, and the doctor was like, "You go to school?"

So we went through testing for a year to see if I was a qualified candidate. It took a year and a half.

Brandon's dad told everybody at their church about it.

On the day of my brain surgery, his dad drove me to the hospital. He says, "Can I pray for you?" I said, "Go ahead." And they prayed for me. Then as I was laying there waiting to be operated on, I felt this warm sensation going through my body. I didn't know what it was. But I know now. It was the Holy Spirit. They started screwing screws into my head, my chest, I was screaming, "Take it off!"

The doctor ignored me. And then I somehow felt the warm feeling going through me. I couldn't explain it. I felt at ease. I caught myself smiling, twiddling my thumbs. And this was while they were drilling my head. The procedure took 10 hours, and I was awake the whole time.

I caught myself staring at my hand—no twitching!

They took me into recovery. The doctor comes in and says, "Can I go out and tell your family they can see you?" I said to the doctor, "I have no family."

Then they opened the door and there were 25 people from the church, 25 people!

There were 25 people who had come just for me.

I guess I do have a family.

I've learned a lot. I've learned to believe in the Lord. Since I became a believer, there is a God, don't underestimate the power of the Lord. I should have been dead a long time ago. I'm determined. If you don't have a family, your church is your family.

****

As we were finishing up our conversation, Wayne's lottery number was called. That meant it was his turn to get his allocation of groceries. This week, he had drawn a low number, meaning that he didn't have a long wait. Instead of going right away to pick up his food, he looked around the room and offered up his low number to another client, a small family, who looked like they might have a hard time waiting. I asked Wayne if he did that often, give up his lower number to someone else.

"Sure," he smiled. "I'm not in a hurry."

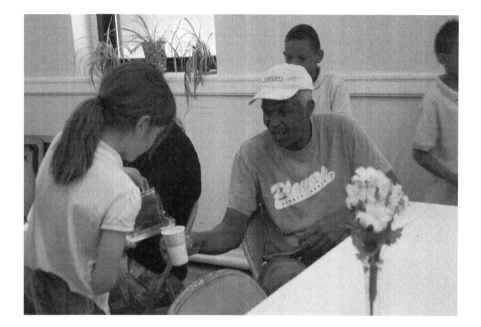

LEONORA

The Chemistry Professor

———

She sits knitting, patiently waiting her turn. Her mastery of knitting radiates a quiet, gentle grace. She has a slight smile, just a hint of amusement in her eyes, as if she is ready to field questions from the colorful blanket she is knitting. You look at her, and before she says a word you think, "What kind of a teacher was she?" You easily imagine her leading a classroom, talking softly, her students leaning in to make sure they catch every word. She communicates much by saying very little. Her eyes alone encourage questions. And there is more: a precision, an order. You wonder if she was a science teacher.

"Leonora?" you begin. "What was your work?"

She looks up. "I was senior professor of chemistry at the University of the Philippines for 30 years."

———

Oh no! I do not talk about myself.

She smiles in a way that communicates both shyness and strength.

I can talk hours and hours about chemistry, but not about myself! In chemistry, there is order. There is beauty. There are rules. There are the students. They talk. The teacher listens, guides.

But to talk of myself? In my country, to talk of oneself is boastful, vain. A woman never speaks of herself. Sometimes I am ashamed to mention it. I studied chemistry. I taught in the college for more than 30 years, the University of The Philippines

Leonora? How many female professors of chemistry were there on staff then?

Well (*she smiles*), there was me.

There was you. What was different about you?

I am an independent woman. Ever since I finished college, age 20. I have always been independent. The way I think. The way I dress. The way I see my life.

Maybe it is in the training of my family. That we should be independent, self-reliant, not a burden to anyone. In the Philippines, the family ties are strong. We care not only for our own children, for all children, our children's children.

Each time she mentions children she smiles. She connects her work in chemistry and in teaching to children. She speaks of chemistry as a way to make sense of the world.

Rather than compartmentalize the different parts of her life, she speaks of the connections in her life.

Everything that I did was connected. I was a mother, a teacher, a chemist, an administrator. We were married and raising children and correcting papers and going to market, and there never was a moment when we were not busy. We were too busy. As teachers, we were always planning lessons, doing administrative work. Perhaps we were so busy that it all flowed together.

What else connected all of it? Connected my life with my children, my students, my country? That's just the way it was. All connected. I helped my husband earn money for the family. Perhaps that is what connected it all? But it was all connected.

We spoke English since we were children. We had a very well-rounded education—linguistics—we had to learn English to communicate. I grew up with a very broad-minded father. My father believed we were all here to think. He'd ask me if I had ever seen this movie or that movie. He didn't know we cut classes to see the movies.

She giggles.

Our high school was in the heart of Manila. We paid only 85 cents for a double feature. And cool! Air-conditioned. In Manila it is very hot! So to refresh ourselves we saw so many American movies. So many movies! We were crazy about Rock Hudson! So surprised when we learned he was gay! I liked Richard Widmark, Charlton Heston in *The Ten Commandments*. The movie *Trapeze* with Burt Lancaster.

Everything American is popular there.

She laughs merrily.

My husband was my boss! He was the dean of the College of Engineering.

Tell me more about your independent thinking.

I was independent thinking every moment when I was married. But I still did the shopping, the cooking. "That is your department," my husband would say to me. It is not what one does. It is what one thinks. In a classroom, one does not just repeat the formulas. That is not thinking. That is talking.

Tell me about your husband. She looks down and her voice becomes even softer.

He was dean of the College of Engineering. A chemist and an engineer. We got married in 1960. Our life was good. We were good. My husband was 10 years older than me. He passed away at age 69. This was seven or eight years ago.

Then I came here to America. My children were here. I've been in Chicago for just under two years. Before I came here I stayed in California. I stayed with the family of my eldest son. He was the one who petitioned to have me emigrate here after my husband passed away.

While in California I was babysitting my grandkids. I did not take any other kind of work. It is a full-time job. The youngest kids I was taking care of were twins. So I had them left and right.

She smiles and brings up her arms as if holding a baby on either side. The ups and downs of a very full life come

through on her face. One can envision the upturned faces
of her chemistry students studiously taking notes.

I was living with my son in California. And one of my daughters just called me. She got a package deal. She was given immigrant visas for her family, or all five of them, three boys, the husband and her. They came to Chicago.

She worked as a nurse at St. Elizabeth Hospital here in Chicago. She was a new mother. My son saw that his sister in Chicago needed me more than he did because her children were small here, so he offered me, "Mama, would you like to help in Chicago?"

So two new grandsons for me! I had two new grandsons and then I developed cancer. Breast cancer. So I was in surgeries. I could not do as much as I was doing.

The talk returns to her children and grandchildren and
she brightens.

Oh, I am happy for my grandchildren. I have 14 of them! I had seven children. Six living. I lost my son to heart disease. But I have 14 grandchildren, six here in the United States.

When I came here to Chicago to again look after my grandchildren—after a while my daughter and her family, they relocated to Texas. She took a job as a nurse there, a better job for her. She was asking me to join them.

The problem with me is that if I stay with any of my children, I keep working and working. This is me, always thinking, always working. Nothing about that has changed since my time at the university or my time as a young mother.

My daughter understood that. She is like me in that way, always working, thinking. So she helped me look for a place to stay because I like it here in Chicago. In Chicago, there is the Common Pantry. I would be hungry if the Pantry was not here in Chicago.

I thought of going back to the Philippines—but I have a history of hypertension, of heart disease. And then the cancer. I didn't like the idea of depending on my children. They have their own family.

In the Philippines now there is no buying power in the peso. Money can't buy a lot. Fifty pesos used to buy food for a family for a week. Now you need thousands! Politics in the Philippines is very frustrating. We have tried all kinds of presidents: old, young, schooled, not schooled, intelligent, not intelligent—they all come out corrupt.

Maybe they learn from you in America? I hear on the TV, corruption in American government.

I never stop being amazed at how big America is! The space here in America! There is so much room! There is food. Oh, compared to the Philippines? Now I hear the prices have gone up. It is the floods. The people are afraid of the water. The ground is cracking and no crops will grow. So that makes it difficult.

I miss it. But it is for survival I stay here. But I'm happy here! I survived the winters here in Chicago!

I have three grandchildren in Dallas. Three in California. But here it is just me.

I am happy in the place I am staying. They take good care of us at St. Vincent de Paul Residence the residence at the back of Martha Washington. They really take good care of us. They are at Irving Park and Western (a ten-minute walk from Common Pantry). I believe it was built eight years or so ago.

I have friends who have gone around the country and they have told me seniors get benefits in Illinois that most seniors do not get. I have talked to people about this, some senior friends in California. The best place for seniors is here. I feel very safe here.

Some friends told me about the Common Pantry. I heard about it at St. Ben's, the Catholic church near here. I saw the Common Pantry address along Damen. And I come by myself.

I need special food for my health. I do not want to call my children for this.

You are proud to take care of yourself.

Oh, sometimes when the snow is not so high I come here too! Not regular because of the weather. We get shampoo and toothpaste here. They do not have those things at other pantries.

And then the people here at this place are so very good. They are very gracious and very dignified.

At this age—I am happy.

Her eyes are bright. Just the way they must have been when she was up in front of her chemistry lectures. Even now while we talk, she knits. She creates.

I remember what George Burns said, "Happiness is having a loving family and living in another state."

If you had to give a message to the Common Pantry, what would it be? What would you say?

I am happy to contribute to this book in any way I can so you can go on with this project. I know how important it is to remember people's stories. And this place, the Common Pantry, helps me, helps other people.

At this age, I am happy.

JAMES
Doing Something Good In Life

———

A slender young man slouches at the table under a faded red baseball cap.. He could be anywhere from 25 to 50 years old. He moves as if he is used to blending into the walls, as if he almost expects to not even be seen.

Yet his grasp of the purpose of this book is instantaneous. If he were in business, he'd be called a "big picture guy."

He speaks of a religious group he's joined. The group is bussed from the Chicago streets to the northwest suburb of Arlington Heights every Sunday morning.

"When I'm part of that group on the bus, going out to that church, I'm part of something larger than myself. I am doing something good in life. And I want to give what I can, I want to contribute, too.

That's what I'm hoping comes of us talking. Maybe by us talking, helping you out by sharing my story for the book, I'm doing something good in life."

———

I'm living on the streets in Uptown and it makes me feel totally insane. Because people are like animals. It makes me feel totally insane. Because on one hand, I don't want to deal with these people. And on the other hand, I want to do something good in life.

Places like the Common Pantry are important! I've been coming here regular ever since I been on the streets. Not sure how long. Maybe five years. I get my food here. I come to the Wednesday night meal. Places like this are important. No B.S.

Tell me about you and working.

People think homeless people don't want to work. That is not true. At least not for me. I worked at U.S. Robotics. That was back in the day when modems were external devices. Now, of course, every computer has a built in modem. It was on the production side. First job was as a production clerk; I liked it. I was there a few years, then they promoted me. I was a production supervisor. Then I was a receiving supervisor. We had a big contract with Apple Computer.

But the industry changed so much. It was so volatile.

When things change so fast, sometimes all you can do is laugh. I was a receiving supervisor and there was basically nothing to receive! So they started laying people off. I was one of the last to go.

I was one of the first 40 employees to work there. I picked up how to do the job while I was on the job. I never had training or anything like that. I learned on my own. The reason I got promoted was that I paid attention. We had some very dedicated customers, and I took care of them: used their labels; customized orders.

I was the guy who everyone would ask, "What do we do with this company? That company?" And I paid attention. Kept track of what was going on. I always tried to take my job seriously.

Then I painted for a while. Houses. Apartments. You name it. I liked that, too. I was a good painter. My daughter was born. And my son was on the way. I wanted a job that provided insurance. And this guy didn't provide that.

Back then Edgewater Hospital (a few miles north of Common Pantry) had a really good medical program—they took real good care of our kids when they were born. But I still needed insurance.

So while I did painting, I was looking for work. Finally, I got a call back from this lighting company, and I was there for five years. Then we were sold to a foreign corporation. People I worked with would always say, "Oh, if you would have been here when Joe owned the company, those were good times." But a European company bought us. Then they started buying up lighting companies all over the country, and they had us competing against each other. Basically, they were greedy.

I see greed all over the place. Not just at companies, everywhere: on the streets, at work, everywhere.

How do you spend your days?

I do a lot of floating around. I'm in this area on Wednesday for the Common Pantry. But I'm also here for the Sulzer Library, just a little north of here. I go there frequently. I was very sad that Chicago reduced the hours of the library. When they do that, they are taking something that's important to a lot of people; well, at least to me. They cut the hours, but still have four security guards that do nothing. They kept the security guards, but they cut the people behind the desk, the people that actually do the work. So now the line goes all the way around the whole place so everybody has to wait longer, so everybody loses; except the security guards who do nothing.

Basically, it makes me pretty angry.

I was brought up in a house where my father would complain about the government a lot. Government this. Government that. And I guess I kind of picked it up, agreeing with him without really knowing why. It's scary. One day you turn around and you're just like your old man!

I was born around Division and Pulaski. It's near the west side, but not quite as far. Growing up, my grandmother owned the house we lived in. She controlled us through her daughter— my mother. When I got married, we moved in with the family. We eventually got out of the house, my wife and I—moved out to be near my work, my work at the lighting company. I was married for about nine years. We had two kids.

When we first got divorced, I used to see my kids every two weeks. That was the court order.

And then I had an accident, an auto accident. Couple months later, she got remarried. Just like that. I guess it was in the works for a while 'cause it happened pretty fast. And so she says to me, "Well, you have to get back on your feet after your accident, so don't worry about the child support."

So I thought, "Oh, well that's good."

But as time went by and I started being able to think more clearly—I had been in and out of a coma since the accident—I began to realize that every time I tried to contact my kids, she would be the one that answered. She would tell me they weren't there. "Try calling back later." Controlling the whole thing. She kept on being a buffer.

And when I would reach one of the kids, just because they'd pick up the phone when I called, they'd end up saying, "Ah . . . I gotta go 'cause Mom's here."

So I finally said to my ex-wife, "I don't understand what happened. Why are you being this way? I've always loved the kids and they've loved me."

It was as if she was trying to pretend I never existed, that we were never married. I told her that if the shoe was on the other foot, I'd always make sure that she'd be able to see the kids.

I don't know why so many things like that happen in life. I mean the fact that my mother died shocked me. I was seven. You know what I mean? I almost lost religion.

Because my mother, she was the one who was in charge. My dad, he was just doing the stereotypical role. He was the breadwinner. But my mother was in charge.

And I never knew she was even ill. No one ever told me. When I tried to ask questions, this was like a rule, they would say, "Children are to be seen and not heard." He was old school. A lot of people say that, but they don't enforce it. In my house, they enforced it. If I didn't shut up when I was told to shut up— then I'd get, you know, smacked.

So one day they said to me, "Mom's in the hospital." I asked why. They said, "Oh, don't worry about it, she's just a little sick." They all went to the hospital. Everyone went but me. I couldn't go. I was like, "What is this? Why can't I go see Mom?"

And then they all came back, they were all sad. And then they said, "Your ma passed away."

I didn't have any reaction. I didn't really even understand it. And then eventually I realized it. I think when I got divorced,

20 years later, that's when I first cried about it. 'Cause I was sad about the divorce, too.

See that? See how I start talking about being married and I end up talking about my mother dying? I guess maybe it's all kind of one subject.

I remember I said to my ex-wife, "I know our marriage isn't really working." But I said to her, "Look, the only way we can fail is if we give up. If we work on this, we can fix the problems that we have." That was another delusion of mine.

I've always been idealistic. Idealism can be a good thing. But only if you can make things happen. That's the thing. I'm not able to make things happen. I can't force anyone to do anything.

What gets you by on the streets?

I'm sorta religious. And I sorta like to use alcohol and drugs when things bother me. So I just go off into my own world, but that gets tiring. That makes it worse. If you're depressed, it makes you more depressed. I been through AA numerous times. Hasn't worked for me.

Tell me about church.

One church I go to strictly is in Arlington Heights.

Every two weeks they bring a bus down to the city and park it across from Wrigley Field. A school bus. They pick up people and they bring them out to the church in Arlington Heights.

It's called Orchard Evangelical Free Church. The way it started was that this woman, she wasn't even religious at the time, she had a son who was in his teens. And he liked to, for whatever reason, help homeless people. And he got into drugs. I don't know how it happened, but he died.

I heard the woman tell it like this. "It was a year after my son had died, it was his birthday. And I prayed to the Lord that I could bake him a cake. And the Lord said, *Bake the cake, and then go give it to a homeless person or a homeless shelter.*"

So she did. She went over to the Lakeview Shelter. And this is how it got started. The church just had a sixth anniversary.

I usually help them clean, help them set up. The church service starts when we get there, 10:30 to 11:30. Then they have this potluck meal, all this beautiful homemade food that people bring. Sometimes someone will buy a pizza or something, but mostly it's homemade. So it's so good.

Then they have a clothing room. A few women come just to run the clothing room. I don't know how they do it all. It's a pretty big operation.

First they had a van to take people out there. Now they have a school bus. They take 50 or 60 people. Then another church in Arlington Heights started taking the overflow people. And that church was also very generous. Around the holidays, they gave gifts for everyone.

Of course I'd still go there if there were no gifts. They thank me for coming! Can you believe that! And I always tell them, I'm the one who should be thanking you! I always tell them that compared to what I experience in Uptown—this is heaven.

Church and Uptown—and when I say "church" I'm talking about all the churches, I'm talking about the Common Pantry, all of the pantries. The difference between church and the streets of Uptown is like the difference between heaven and hell.

What happens in these places like the Common Pantry is that they fill a big hole in my life. Because I don't associate with my family, my cousins, my siblings, my kids. Both my parents have passed away. I don't know whatever happened to my cousins.

When we were young, my mother used to organize things, get everybody together for family events, holidays, birthdays. But when she died, slowly but surely all that started going away. Everything was gone. Our whole social structure just disintegrated. So we would still get together at Christmas every year, not knowing why, feeling like we were obligated. You could just feel the tension. Everybody would say, "Hey! Merry Christmas! How are you?" But no one really felt it anymore.

So the Common Pantry here fills a hole in my life.

The other side of the story is Uptown, the streets. It's scary. People are like animals. Once when people were lining up for the bus to go out to the church in Arlington Heights, they started in asking and begging for bus passes. "I need a bus pass! I need a bus pass!" Because she gives away bus passes. She gives away lots of things. And she was so patient. Telling them that if they come out to church, she'll give them a bus pass when we get back to Chicago. But they kept after her.

So finally I just had to walk away. That's the part that makes me want to just be left alone. It makes me feel totally insane. Because on one hand, I don't want to deal with these people. And on the other hand, I want to do something good in life.

When I'm part of that group on the bus, going out to that church, everything that happens there—I am doing something good in life. At the Common Pantry, when I am part of something, I am doing something good in life.

But that bus ride is only once every two weeks. The Pantry, that's once every few weeks. Another pantry had an art show once and I was part of that. So most of the time I am not doing something good. When I am in Uptown, I'm not doing anything good.

I feel that everything that happens in my life is for a reason. And all that I'm learning is, I'm like a rat. Because I don't have a full-time job I don't have insurance. If I try and go to an emergency room, even if I'm really sick, they're like, "You don't have insurance?" And you can almost feel the kick in your ass.

Even if I try and use a telephone somewhere, whoever is there—a receptionist maybe—they're like "Hey! Hey!" and you can almost feel yourself being pushed away.

And I really have gotten to the point where I want to be left alone. I don't want to deal with it all.

The way I'm able to get money on occasion is to do flyers. There are 10 to 15 vans that come out, pick us up, and take us to where we pass out flyers house to house. Of course a lot of the people involved with that are not very nice people.

Is there anybody I can trust on the street? Maybe one guy. Maybe a couple more. This one guy, he comes here occasionally. He's from Wisconsin, an ex-CPA.

And I want to give what I can, I want to contribute, too. That's what I'm hoping comes of us talking.

You mentioned doing art and didn't finish the story.

Oh, the art show. Yeah, I just thought about that because it was a bit like what we're doing here. Making a book of all our stories. Only they did it this one time with art.

There is another pantry and church like this one. It's called All Saints Church, over on Wilson and Hermitage. And they had this art project. They gave people a place to display their art. They even offered it up for sale.

I didn't have any art supplies. So what I did was, I found a picture frame in the alley back of the Salvation Army, and a poster from the Chicago Fire soccer team. I had an idea: I tore around the middle to get the logo out. Then I singed the sides of the pennant, so you know, it looked like it had been in a fire. I made it look like it had come from the [Great] Chicago Fire. Then I went on the computer at the library, found pictures and stories of the [Great] Chicago Fire, and made a collage. And put it into this picture frame.

They put it up at All Saints Church. The woman there, Fran, told me that it looked pretty cool. I didn't get a chance to see it because it was the week I go out to Arlington Heights, but they told me that a lot of people came through.

No one bought anything. They asked me how much they should charge for it *(laughs)* I said, "I don't know! It's up to you guys!" Nobody bought anything anyway. But a lot of people saw it. And I would have given the money to the church anyway.

That was a good time. But there are bad times, too, times I feel insane.

Tell me about that.

I think my insanity is a test. The Lord is testing my faith. And I have to believe that everything is going to be all right. Everything is going to be okay even though I can be the biggest idiot in the world.

What matters most in the insane times?

Beer. The insane times are those times when nothing matters to me more than getting another beer. It's a sickness.

You have to go through that alone?

For a while, the last six months, there were a lot of us from the church in Arlington Heights emailing each other. But then I started feeling that I needed to back off for a while and let these people live their lives. Maybe they were answering my emails just to be polite. Sometimes I did that. Maybe they didn't really mean it; hard to tell with an email.

I spend so much time on the computer. But I'm just playing around, playing games, listening to music. I mean if I was working, I could be really productive.

It feels so good to get some of this off my chest. I don't associate with a lot of people. And I really believe that if a person knows how to listen, they can learn. But a lot of what I've been learning has been scaring me.

There's a lot of people on the street who are goofy. I mean, I'm goofy. But these people are scary goofy. There's one of them, I ran into him yesterday. Scary goofy guys who like to fight are the ones you need to watch out for.

The good things in my life just happen. Things like the art. I don't give myself any credit. Everything that's good in my life, the Lord has guided me there.

At the lighting company, I was really into quality control. They let me take a course. I took a course at the American Society for Quality Control.

What's next for you?

I don't know what's next. When I got evicted from my room, that was years ago—I don't really remember why I was evicted, but I was. Not even sure when it was.

As for jobs? If I wanted to be committed to the flyer guys, that would be a steady income, or at least a semi-steady income.

I don't want to do that, though, because the first thing I do? I go back to the liquor store. I feel so humiliated. Passing out flyers: that's a kid's job, not a grown man's job. This is the best I can do? I feel really disappointed in myself. It's kind of like a circle.

At least when I go to the liquor store, it's not drugs. There's other people, addicted to crack, and they're not dealing with people behind a counter in a liquor store who are nice, ask you how you're doing, and then give you your change back. When you are addicted to drugs, you only deal with criminals.

I miss my kids. But what am I gonna tell them? That I've been living on the streets for the past five years? I'm a drunk?

I'm cynical. I don't want to deal with people.

I don't know if there is a way for me to stop.

It's like when I had jobs. I always started out well, but then I'd learn about the company, the politics, and the bad ethics. And that would get to my performance. Make me not want to try.

But a lot of my prayers have been answered. In all those times, I get to sit and talk with people. Not watching the clock, sitting there doing some boring, repetitive thing, just getting to talk to people like right now. Those are answered prayers.

What would be an ideal situation for you?

I'd like to be a janitor for a big building. Be on call to come help people. I can fix pretty much anything. Not rushing. Spending time with people. Fixing things for people. As long as I get it done in the course of the day. Spending time talking with good people.

Kind of like we're doing right now.

This was therapeutic for me!

CARL
The Actor

———

Carl offers an observation that holds true for every single story in this collection. There are no clichés here.

Like with Carl when he said, "So there I was underneath Barbra Streisand's piano. And she is like right here with me. We're on all fours, face to face, inches apart. I'm looking into her nostrils."

Anyone expect to hear that?

Is this a Common Pantry story? Yes, it is. Listen to the story. Enjoy the skills of a practiced actor as he begins entertaining, then as he gets more comfortable, starts delving into his own, unique vulnerability. And perhaps in revealing his vulnerability, Carl offers the insight that all of us—in our own unique way—are also vulnerable.

———

Sure, I know the stories!

And as he says the words, Carl's eyebrows go up and he laughs in a way that brings you into the story, weaving the words with his facial expressions, his hands, using his whole body to communicate. Suddenly, you are looking across the table at Groucho Marx.

Hah! I know all of the stories! The names! I know where all the bodies are buried! Yes, yes, yes! Of course I do!

Where do you want to start? Let's start at the beginning!

I grew up in the Back of the Yards neighborhood, 55th and Ashland. Polish neighborhood. Good neighborhood. Good, hardworking people.

But there was this dream.

He flicks his imaginary cigar ashes. Raises his eyebrows and you say "What dream, Groucho?"

The picture business! Like you couldn't tell that already.

I moved to L.A. and wanted to get a job in the picture business. But I thought, while you're doing that, trying to get your Oscar nomination, you got to have a place to live and a job. Right?

This was in the time that the Persians, the Iranians, lots of folks from the Middle East, were coming to the United States. And I had experience selling Persian rugs here in Chicago. At Marshall Field's, I actually opened the Persian rug department at the Field's store in Water Tower Place.

So when I got to L.A., I went looking for stores that sold Persian rugs. I found one on Wilshire Boulevard. This was February of 1979. Snow and cold at home, but not where I was now! The store was right across the street from the Academy of Motion Picture Arts and Sciences, so I was closer to the dream than ever!

I walked into this gorgeous store, this breathtaking store, resplendent in all the colors, the textures of Persian rugs. I saw these guys sitting in the back, huddled around a little table sipping tea.

And I was a little nervous. Especially back then. I had just got off the jet from Chicago. And I thought, my goodness, Arabs! So I walked up to them and I said, "Good afternoon. I'm looking for a job."

One of them answers me *(in flawless Arab accent)* "Good afternoon. What kind of job do you seek?" And I said, "Well, I sold Persian Rugs in Chicago."

There was a stack of rugs next to one of the gentleman. He held out a hand, pointing with one finger ,and said "Vat kind of rug iz dis?" I was nervous, I said, "I think that it is a Tabriz?" And he said, "No, is Shiraz. But you start tomorrow 9:00 a.m. anyway."

So help me, that's what happened. Are you ready for that?

So I get the job. Now I need an apartment.

I'm talking with these two guys in the back of their store and they say, "We have a friend, a Mr. Yamin. He has furnished apartments on Doheny Drive. Go see him."

It was a classical Art Deco building on Doheny and it was like $250 a month. Furnished.

Inside, the unit was falling apart. It was decrepit. The plaster was crumbling all over the tacky sea green wall-to-wall carpeting. Parts of the ceiling were down; electric cords, peeling paint. It was filthy.

But it was Beverly Hills 90210, so I looked past it. Past the whole thing. A man of vision I was! I could see what it could be.

So I said, "Mr. Yamin how much is it?" And he said, "Iz $300. First and last month rent.'" I said, "Mr. Yamin, I have $500 on me. Can I get it for $250, and I'll give you the other $250 right now?"

He says, "Give to me the cash! God bless you! Good luck! Good luck! Zank you very much!" Then, whoosh! Like the wind he got in his Mercedes.

I yelled, "Mr. Yamin!, I need a receipt!" And he yelled out the window as he drove away, "Ah! I give to you. I bring! I bring to you!"

So I moved into the building.

One thing led to another. Started doing extra work. bit parts. Got to know a few people. Worked every day in the rug store. And the people who'd come in and out! Remember, we're across the street from the Academy of Motion Picture Arts and Sciences. Everyone walked by that store. And some even came in!

Like this one day. This couple, they look like real schleppers, they shuffle through the front door. Little old Jewish couple, they walk into the store, they had been jogging, and they came in to pick out a few rugs. So they decide what they want. And I was asked to go to the home with the Israeli driver to deliver the rugs. Now obviously, these were not poor people, but they looked live real schleppers.

Later on that day we load up the truck and off we go. So we're approaching the address, we pull up and turn into the most breathtaking home on all of Doheny Road.

Out front of this mansion, the houseman, an African-American gentleman in a starched white jacket, is playing Frisbee on the wide sweeping green lawn with some kids.

We ring the door chime. Margo Winkler, the lady of the house, answers the door and says, "Come on in darling! Want an Oreo cookie? We're taking the rugs into the projection room!"

First projection room I had ever been in my life; it was as big as the whole downstairs of this church. Enormous. And everything was white. White tiles. White walls. White windows. White, white, white. With some plants.

So we're putting these colorful handmade Persian rugs, on the floors. White fireplace, white mantle. The only things in the room that had any color at all, till we started putting down these rugs, were these mugs on the bar. Golden mugs. And on each mug, engraved, were the names of the husband's films. One on each mug.

The husband was a producer. There were the names of all his films, and there were lots of them, engraved on these mugs.

I look on the mantle, and there is a gold statue of a man holding a sword on a reel of film. And I said to myself, "Self, that's an Oscar."

So, I walked up to it and I read the base: Awarded to Irwin Winkler. Producer. Best Picture of the Year. ROCKY.

You know the director, John Avildsen, was from Oak Park. But this was Irwin Winkler. The producer.

So now I'm kind of moving in these circles. It was fascinating. Of course you know they make these little trophies, these Oscars, on the northwest side of Chicago. Bryn Mawr and Elston. Always a Chicago connection!

He takes a breath. His first in a couple of minutes.

Okay, so a few weeks later, a woman comes in the store. I was out for lunch at the time. But she picks out some rugs, says "Have them delivered, we want to see how they'll look at the house." So the next morning, I come in, and they say, "You go with Youseef. Your English is better. You go. You go to Barbra Streisand house. Don't ask for autograph. Just go. Be nice!"

So we take off, and I get lost in Benedict Canyon. I'm new, just a kid from Back of the Yards in Chicago, trying to work his way around Beverly Hills. Youseef is just in from Israel. And we just could not find that house.

So finally I pulled over. I asked a Bel Air patrolman, "Do you know where this house is?" I mean we had the address, the directions, but we just could not find this house.

And he said, "Okay, go this way, that way, turn here than turn there, than go two blocks and you'll see the house with the gray tarp." Very confusing. And I said, "So, you can't take us there?"

And they say no—we don't do that.

So eventually we found the place, we get to the house, pull up, Margarita answers the buzzer, she says, "Okay," and we go in. It's this gorgeous English thatched home. Breathtakingly beautiful. From the 1920s. Found out later that the original owner was Greta Garbo.

And a lovely short Jewish woman with flowing brown air, awesome skin and "the Nose" answers the door. It's Barbra.

She says, "What happened to you guys! You're late!"

And I said, "I am so very sorry. I'm Carl."

And she says, "My name is Barbra."

Can you believe that's what she said! Yes, I know it's the name of one of her most famous albums. But that is what she said! "My name is Barbra!" And I'm thinking, "Yeah, I know."

So we go into the music room—I'm glad you're sitting down for what's coming—and the first thing we have to do is roll up these tacky area rugs. These tacky, cheap rugs that are on wall-to-wall rose carpet. And the music room is like, it's got a balcony up there running along one side of it. You could do a scene from Romeo and Juliet. Breathtakingly beautiful room, exquisite, looking out on the lawns and the pool, and there is a baby grand piano.

So the first place Barbra wants to try the rugs out is under the piano. Youseef, you know, the big Israeli guy who was with me, and some other big guy who worked for Barbra doing something, I do not know what, they start lifting the piano.

I get on all fours with Barbra, and we crawl under the piano, we pull the rugs out while the guys lift this piano.

Face to face, inches apart, we're on all fours, I'm looking into her nostrils. The most famous nose in the world, I guess, after, what, Jimmy Durante?

So now we get the rugs arranged around the room. This way. That way. A little to the left. And in strolls her designer "Costa."

Costa starts walking around, giving us directions on switching out rugs. Rearranging everything. He's muttering, "No, not this one, no, not this, umm, no, no, no."

And they didn't like any of the rugs. None of them. *None* of them.

She shrugs her shoulders, says, "I'm sorry. We didn't like any of the rugs." She was very nice. But I thought it was very odd that she didn't like any of them. I was there from like 10:00 in the morning till 1:30 in the afternoon. She says, "Tell your boss, we'll be in again."

But I spent a lot of time there and I thought, gee, some kind of tip. Something? Anything? Nothing.

That's a great story. So what was life like out in Hollywood?

I did it all out there. The bit parts. The auditions. The bad jobs. The good jobs. I managed the building I lived in. I know *all* the stories! Hell, I did stand-up for 12 years. I was out there for 24 years.

That is a long time, 24 years. What brought you home to Chicago? And as he begins to talk about coming home, his pace slows.

A friend of mine had lost her father and she said, "Carl, I would give anything to have one more day with my dad. Go home Carl." My folks were getting elderly. The neighborhood had changed. My folks had moved to Lincoln Park. I was getting phone calls from them late at night. I started getting anxiety attacks.

His pace drops again. He is no longer entertaining. He is telling his story.

So I sold everything, cleaned out the closets, shipped everything, and came back here.

If you don't have an Oscar nomination after 24 years, go home. Go back to Boise, or Milwaukee, or Chicago. So I came home.

I came home and I had my parents for about one year together. My dad passed away, September 2, 2004. He had been ill.

I was working for Marshall Field's again, downtown. And I walked into the store one morning through the employee entrance, mid-October. And I saw the sign: Visit the Tree Shop on the 9th Floor. Christmas is coming. And I thought, well, my father is gone, thank goodness I still have my mother, and she'll be here for the holidays.

October 20, the phone rings in my apartment on North Damen Avenue. It goes to the machine. I got the call. I checked the message about an hour later. It was my sister, Gerilyn. "Carl, call me as soon as you get this message." And I knew, I knew when I heard that message, I knew my mom was gone, I knew she had joined my dad.

I called my sister. My hand was shaking. I dialed a wrong number, then I got her, and she said it: "Carl, Mom's gone."

I knew she didn't mean Mom was taking a walk around the neighborhood.

So, two parents in seven weeks. I have not been the same since.

I fell into a serious funk. Depression. I lost a good job, Nordstrom's, North Michigan Avenue. I was an independent contractor working for the fragrance distributors. Now, that business is gone. Dried up. Nobody is buying a bottle of Prada for men for $90.00. They go to CVS and get Mennen for $4.99 a bottle.

So I fell into this depression. I've been in therapy ever since. I have a good therapist.

Anti-depressants really don't work. A good friend of mine said, "You're suffering from a situational depression." A doctor at Cook County said, *(in a German accent as Carl the entertainer surfaces again)* "You have an existential depression. You have what we refer to in the profession as an existential depression."

Carl laughs.

So thank God I went to school and actually know what that means!

I spoke to a woman at a brunch I went to one day, and she said, "You are mourning your life." Truer words were never spoken. I'm not joking. And neither was she.

So here I am. Hitting the skids. Down and out.

Living on Damen. Was on unemployment, but that just ran out. No enjoyment, only annoyment when you're on unemployment.

I come here, to the Common Pantry, periodically, for back up. I get food stamps. That's it. I call the State of Illinois film production number every week, but there really is no work. Nothing is going on.

I hear your depression, and believe it. Everything you are saying about the depression rings so very true. You're also one of the most entertaining people I've ever met. I haven't laughed this much in a long time. How can a guy who is so funny and entertaining also be so depressed?

Here's the thing about depression: When I think about all these wonderful times, I'm an actor. That means that I can go there, experience it, and I can convey it. But when I go home, and close my apartment door, I can sit and cry for hours.

So you have a sense of how talented you are?

No, not at all. The greatest actors in Hollywood don't have a clue. And the ones who have no talent think that they do.

I've been like this all my life. This is my personality. But the blow of losing my family . . . One therapist said to me, "I believe your family must have communicated through stories because you have the greatest stories."

My answer? Well. Of course! The film studios, all of them, they were built by people telling stories. Not group therapy. Stories.

When people first discovered fire, when people first started cooking food, they would sit around the fire and tell the stories of the hunt. This is how all socialization started. That came first. Stories came first. Not questions on how a person feels. Stories.

I've been around all the great acting teachers. Susan Strasberg, I knew her. Nice girl. Died of breast cancer. She was Kim Novak's sister in the film version of *Picnic*.

Isn't Kim Novak from Chicago, too?

Yes, she is. From Montrose and Hermitage. Her real name is Marilyn.

Her Dad was a conductor for the Chicago and North Western Railroad. But when she went to Hollywood, Harry Cohn, who was the head of the studio said to her, "If you're gonna work for Columbia pictures, your name is gonna be Kim Novak. Darryl Zanuck's already got a Marilyn, Marilyn Monroe, so I can't have Marilyn Novak. From now on you are Kim!"

See what happens? Out there in Hollywood, they can even take your name if they want.

And there is depression there. Depression here. I know that.

But there are also stories. Good ones. The stories keep us going.

Stories? You want stories?

I could go on forever with the stories.

MARIE
Rainbow Lady

———

Marie is a slender woman in a muted multi-colored raincoat buttoned up tight to the top. She radiates an almost musical energy. She speaks very quickly, changing subjects in a blink. There is a staccato rhythm in her voice. Her eyes dart around the room.

She has fought some battles. She skims over her struggles like a stone skipping across the waves. If certainty and stability and calm are your preference, she could make you nervous, put you off your guard. But if you're open to stories of what it means to survive, she is a treasure.

She is proud of the rings on her fingers. She begins by talking about those rings. The sentences pour out fast. She looks around the room as she speaks.

———

This one I got at T. J. Maxx. This one I got at a thrift store. This one I got at a place on Devon Avenue. This one I got at the Sweden Shop. They call me the Rainbow Lady at all the thrift stores. They all know me at all the places I go. Everybody calls me the Rainbow Lady because I like different colors: purple, pink, yellow, orange, green. Like rainbows!

"Look," they say. "Here she comes! Here comes the Rainbow Lady!"

She smiles. You like being different from other people, don't you? What were you like when you were 13?

I've always wanted to live life like I wanted. Even back when I was 13, I wanted so badly to be 10. I didn't want to get any older. I wanted to be 10.

If we had a picture of you at 10 years old sitting right here on the table, what would it look like?

I dressed like a cowgirl. I saw Western movies, lots of movies. You'd see me all dressed up in pigtails, smiling, in a little cowgirl outfit. I loved the movies.

This was the mid-1950s then, right?

Right! Yes!

Tell me about you and the movies.

I'd pretend that it was me in the movies. I dreamed it was me. It was me running away. I wanted so badly to be a princess or to be a cowgirl. Running away with a big handsome cowboy on a horse. A prince in a carriage. A royal prince. Of course he had to be somebody that I really liked. Somebody that I really liked a lot. I loved the movies because I loved living inside the fairy tales. Westerns I loved. Musicals. Like *Carousel* and *Oklahoma*. I never wanted to leave those movies.

Tell me what you wanted to happen when you were living in those movies.

I would dream of meeting a Prince Charming on a white horse. A smiling face that I could bring home to dinner. But a smiling face I really liked.

And it never turned out that way because I always attracted the wrong people. I made so many mistakes. I just picked anybody with a pretty smile, a nice face. It didn't turn out that way for me.

Even when I graduated from grammar school I hid behind the curtains instead of marching down the aisle. I don't know why I did that. I would never do that now. But I wasn't as smart as I am now. I learned from living. I let people take advantage of me. If somebody said they'd beat me up, I'd hide in the house for two days. I was scared to go to school. They'd call on me to recite something. I'd hide.

Her voice turns stronger, defiant.

Now? Now I'd march right down that aisle and stand up proudly!

You sound ready to fight at any time. That's a lot different from living in the movies.

I've changed. Now I've lived through so many experiences. Everywhere I've ever lived, people have wanted me out. That's the main thing about me. People always want me to leave.

What was it like when you were very little?

My mother and father and I, we used to argue. We all used to scream. Everybody would always want us out. We weren't like the other families.

We were different.

I guess misery loves company. That's what changed. Too many things have happened now.

You were different as a child. But also as an adult. What made you different as an adult?

Maybe it started with the baby, my first baby. I had a baby, and her arm was missing. She was born without the arm.

I was in shock. I couldn't have people come up to me and say, "Oh, I'm so sorry." I couldn't have that. So I hid. I hid. And I used to take long walks with her. And I'd cover up her arm. We'd walk and we'd walk. We'd spend the day walking. I was 23.

Did you know why she was born without the arm?

They'd tell me it was my fault. That it was genetics. But it was a drug. They had given me this diet pill, Preludin. That's what did it.

(Note: Preludin was declared unsafe and taken off the market in 1965. The link to birth defects is referenced in the medical literature.)

I just couldn't face reality anymore. I listened to the doctor. I believed the doctor. They told me I could have ten more babies. But I didn't know.

I had another daughter, a son, and then another daughter. And they were all right. But I just couldn't get over my first child. And as she grew up, I said a lot of bad things to her. And as she grew up, she got on drugs, prescription drugs. We got off to the wrong start. I didn't mean to call her names. I didn't know what I was doing. Now I live with the guilt.

She died about a year ago. She died young. She smoked. It was cancer that got her. Not the drugs. It was cancer.

What would you say to her if you could talk to her right now?

I'd say, "Laura, I love you. I didn't mean to say all the things I said to you. No one ever taught me right from wrong. I didn't know."

I learned though. My other daughter, she's going to be a teacher. She lives near me. She's just about to graduate. She's burned out from working, but she's going to graduate. I am so proud of her!

Did you have friends as a young woman?

Back then, I had a friend, Phyllis. She was a true friend. We'd go out to eat together. We'd pay for ourselves. Yes, sir, I could always pay for myself.

And we'd go dancing. The Aragon Ballroom, back then it was beautiful. Magical. Like a castle. Italian boys liked to go to the Aragon. We liked that. We'd go see Chuck Foster and his big band. Probably no one remembers Chuck Foster, but I remember him.

We saw all the bands. The Aragon really was a magic place. It was like a Spanish castle. I could live in that castle. Maybe it was a little bit like the movies I used to go to when I was little.

And the Vogue Ballroom, it was a movie theater and a ballroom. That's gone now. It was on Broadway near Halsted and Grace. We'd go there, too. We knew all the places.

I always loved music, all kinds of music. Connie Francis, she'd sing, "Where the Boys Are." Patsy Cline, I loved her. Sad songs, she'd sing sad songs like "Walkin' After Midnight."

I sing all the time. I play the kazoo. I feel the music in my mind and I can play it.

It just comes to me. I can play anything. I feel it. I have a short attention span, but I can feel the vibrations of the music. Back then, I even started square dancing!

Now, now I've changed a lot. I don't care for any of the movies. Now I like real things. Criminal investigations. Criminal justice. Not *CSI*. Not *Law and Order*. None of that stuff is really true. I like true crime. Real things that happen.

Now I take care of myself. I follow the rules. Just tell me what to do, I do it. I stand up to people, but I follow the rules.

I don't eat garbage. I take care of myself. That's why we come here, to the Common Pantry. The food, it's healthy here. How long have we been coming? I don't know, maybe a year or so. You hear about this place on the street. A friend told me. I don't always need food, but I have friends who do, so I help them. My guy, my Eddie, sometimes I come with him and he gets food.

Are you religious?

No religion, I don't believe in religion. I never went to any kind of church. I don't believe in robbing somebody on Saturday and going to church on Sunday. Just don't break the rules! A good person helps people—if they have a lot of money, they give it. Go to school. Don't break the law. Don't steal.

What does it mean to be a good person?

Somebody who helps someone and doesn't ask for anything in return. That's a good person.

What keeps me going? He does.

She points off at the man sitting and smiling drinking coffee in the larger room next door.

Eddie.

Eddie smiles. Nods. Says nothing. Asked if he'd like to be interviewed, he made it clear with the shake of a head that Marie does the talking for the couple. And he is more than fine with that. She continues to speak of Eddie as he sits patiently in the large hall outside the Sunday School room where the interviews take place.

We've been together almost 19 years. He's a good man. Sometimes he's too nice. I try to get him to stand up for his rights.

We're always running, Eddie and me. You'll never catch us stopping for nobody or nothing. We like to be on the move.

We go to the VFW, the fish fry. Eddie was in the war. He's the commander of the post. We both collect stuff. *(She laughs.)* We're hoarders. Thrift shops. Knick-knacks. I collect butterflies. Different color ones, of course!

She smiles big.

That's why they call me the Rainbow Lady!

You got to stand up for yourself. Somebody pushes, you push back. Sure, I've been in some fights. We could talk hours about that.

But you stand up for yourself. You don't let anyone mess with you. And you follow the rules.

Like here: You get your number for the food. You wait nicely. You don't get in no one else's business. They got nice people working here. I respect that.

TOM
A Working Man

———

Look hard at Tom. Because if you don't, you'll miss him. He speaks in fragments of thoughts. The connections between fragments seem vague. Choppy. As you listen hard, you'll realize that there are unspoken messages here, too.

Tom begins hesitantly. Softly, with a trace of an Irish brogue. A slender, gray-haired man in a red baseball cap with a scrubbed clean pink face, he often looks down, not making eye contact.

The conversation begins with his embarrassed admission that the building where he rents a room had been struck by bed bugs. But there's another message. Unsaid. The message is shame. You feel his shame.

Then another seemingly unconnected fragment: He's grateful. The man with the bedbugs is grateful.

Without the Common Pantry, he'd be hungry. He, a man who has worked hard all his life, would be hungry. Unspoken, added to the shame, and to his gratefulness, is bewilderment. He worked hard all his life and, although he's grateful, he's not sure why life turned out the way it did.

He followed all the rules. He did what he was supposed to do. He took one step after another. He tried to do good. He was a workingman with dignity. And now: bedbugs, bewilderment and gratefulness.

———

It was Galway we came from. Leaving from County Cork. That's where all the ships came from, County Cork. Galway though, Galway was our family home. Galway was green and beautiful as far as the eye could see. And every time it rained, the land just got more green.

I was 12 when I came here. Came with my parents. This was in the early 1950s, I would say. Times were bad back then. More money to be made here in America. Lot of Irish was coming over. We came for the money. For the work.

My father was in construction. Four sisters. Three brothers. Always the big families for the Irish. *(He laughs.)* We wanted to build an army to fight the English. That's why we're making so much family.

We came first to South Boston. So first, we were Southies. Not too long did we stay there. My father knew people here in Chicago. The north side of Chicago. Lakeview. Lakeview was nice then. Different families. Germans, Swedes, little bit of everything.

I kept to myself. Just like any other kid. Hard time in the beginning because I came from another country. We spoke the Gaelic. English, too. At that time, they wanted to forget about the Gaelic. Everything was about English. English would be better to get along here. Course now Gaelic is coming back in Ireland. They even teach it in school.

I grew up pretty good. I had friends. Always had friends. On the poor side, we were.

My mother was a hearty woman. She had also lost a few kids. Some tough times.

My father. He was a good-hearted workingman. He died when he was younger, 62. What got to the old man? Cancer.

The old man liked his Guinness.

What did I do for fun? Me and my buddies, we'd go to social dances. Maybe have a few beers on the side.

I was fair at school. I was pretty good at spelling. School was good.

I had to get out of high school though to get some work. There was a lot of work at that time when you turned a certain age. All the factories, the bakeries along Ravenswood Avenue, everything. A lot going on. There was a lot of work.

But it was kinda stupid on my part for dropping out of school. My mother didn't go for it. Telling the old man, "What he do? Drop out of school?" There was some talking when I did that.

Wasn't just me though. There was a lotta other ones dropping out of school. Course school back then, as long as you got out of grammar school, you were okay. School was different back then. I went to Lake View High School. I did my time in school.

After I left school, after I left Lake View, I worked all my life. I really did.

It's when he talks about work that the substance of his life starts to unfold. Tom is one of the unsung men of the neighborhood who simply worked hard. He was the guy who made sure that the trucks were loaded, the shelves stocked, the floors cleaned, all of those jobs that are never celebrated but are always needed.

I had some good jobs and some bad ones.

Best one? I worked at the Merchandise Mart. They were paying good, real good. Loading on the docks, that's what I did. It was good. You know, that building was owned by the Kennedys. Irish. Still is run by the Kennedy family, one of the sons, son of Bobby. All those Kennedys were handsome young men.

I had some other good jobs, too. Worked for United Stationers Supply Company. You know stationery? Pencils, pens. They used to be on Lake and Des Plaines. They had a big warehouse there. Big, big place. I started out being an order filler, pushing big carts around. They kinda give you a little promotion. Make you a section man. That was in the stock department. A little bit of a raise. Not much, but something.

Growing up, we lived on Damen and Belmont. That was all right. When I moved out of my family's house, I lived in Uptown. Lot of Southern people there. I fell right in with them. They were workers. Good people.

I've done factory, clean up, construction. If it's work, I've done it. Along the way, sure there were hard times. Everybody has hard times. That's why the Common Pantry helps.

Everybody has hard times. Like me and the polio.

I was here about two years and I caught polio. Managed to live with it. Had to live with it. Maybe there was other work I could have done without the polio. Maybe I could have gotten a good job in construction. But there was certain work I couldn't do. Lifting up above your head, that kinda thing. I was crippled for about five months one time. Couldn't get out of bed. I got treatments from the hospitals, big hot tubs. I was in Cook County when I was contagious. Then they shipped me to Children's Memorial. I got some good care. I was in a wheelchair for a while.

But that was good because it meant I was close to walking. That was good. And then after that, I was walking. But that wasn't so bad. And I got right back to work. After the polio, I got right back to work.

And the talk of deeper trials leads to family. Leads to marriage.

I never had been married. But I had been with a woman for a long, long time - good 18 years. We was the best of friends. We coulda got married. But she had her own thing going. She had family on her part. She moved in with me for a while. Everything was going good . . . .

Tom pauses and looks off into the distance.

She passed away. That was back say about a good . . .oh I guess it was in the 90s.

Most important thing to know about me? I'm a good person. I always like to, to look for someone, look around to see if anybody . . . if anybody needs help. Every place I ever worked, all the factories, everywhere, I always try to do extra. I look out for the older people. Had some older people, did some work for them, shoveling snow . . . garden work. Kept me busy.

I go to church once in a while. I go to St. Ben's. I been to Epiphany Church, too. I always been a believer in my head. You don't have to be a churchgoer. It's in yourself. It's what you do. What they do here in this church . . . it's nice. It's good. I'm glad to have this place, this Pantry. Wednesday night and the good dinner they got here, it's a real nice place. Couldn't say for sure how long I've been coming. Not sure what I'd do without it.

I don't like to not be busy. When you're not doing nothing, when you ain't got nothing in your pockets? It gets you down . . . you get a little bit of . . . it gets you down.

And when he looks out at how the neighborhood has changed during his lifetime, the comments, as always, return to work.

Used to be that people who got work, got good jobs with the city, only helped their own kind. That's still going on. Maybe not as much.

Who am I?

I'm a good guy. A good person. Hard worker. Honest person. I do my best. I work hard. I try to help.

LAUREN
From the Neighborhood

She is a substantial woman most often dressed in purple, her various IDs and her CTA pass hung like necklaces around her neck.

She's a regular. Sometimes for food from the Common Pantry. Sometimes just for the Wednesday night meal, and sometimes just for warmth, protection from the elements and conversation. Because in living on the street that week she has no place to store the food. The constant is that she is part of the neighborhood.

Given the freedom to talk about what's most important to her, there are of course gaps in her story, as there would be for any of us. The gaps offer the listener the gift of humility, a reminder that we never really know the whole of a neighbor's story.

We don't know the exact nature of Lauren's disability. She reports always being poor, but we don't know what she did when she did work. We know her sense of isolation from other young mothers as they talked of their children, but we don't know any of the specifics. We only know that the isolation was painful. We know the important part, but we don't know it all. That's where the humility comes in. With the gaps in the story, we never know it all.

So instead of trying to fill those gaps, we listen, no matter what the gaps, no matter what seems to not make sense. We find that a conversation with Lauren can take one literally anywhere. Like today, when she began by talking about the American psychologist Dr. Abraham Maslow.

———

Abraham Maslow. I studied him. Read all of his work. He said that we have to feel safe, feel secure. Then you need food. Maybe I come here because I feel safe.

I feel bad for children fighting. Really bad. They do not understand their strength. They could knock out an eye. They could kill someone. But they do not know their strength. So feeling safe is not easy.

I was born in Chicago and a few days later my mother was asked to move. Eviction. This was at Buena and Broadway. So I started out by being evicted.

My mother wasn't married. My father dated her till she was pregnant. Told her he was going to marry her. They got engaged. And then she found out he had another wife.

So this was my first experience with eviction. We left, my mother and I.

It was shameful, at that time, 50 years ago, it was shameful for a woman to have a child on her own. Women wearing short sleeves or no sleeves, even that was controversial. Very different for women back then, so my mother did not have it easy.

I grew up in Logan Square. A nice neighborhood. Mostly a white neighborhood. Some Mexicans. Puerto Ricans. African-Americans.

Very first thing I remember myself is throwing something out a window. An eggbeater. Laughing. Throwing things out the window!

Kids had some fights because that's what kids do, but mostly everybody seemed to get along. A really nice neighborhood.

I got along with people. Except for this one girl. There was this one girl who always wanted to beat me up. I don't know what was going on with her. Probably something in her family. I didn't understand that then. But she used to beat me up. And one time when I was cowering from her I accidently stepped on her sandal and saw that she felt powerless. And that's when I really learned how to fight. I was about four. All of this I figured out by mistake. I stepped on her sandal, she was powerless.

Then I turned aggressor.

I've had physical fights. When I lived in the shelters, I was attacked a lot. I asked people, why me? And they told me it was because I was smart. And they don't like it when you're smart. So I became an aggressor.

Fighting is everywhere. One time a guy appears at my spot on the street, my bus shelter, and says he's gonna stay there with me. I said, "No you're not! Everybody knows this is my spot. The cops know it. The people in the neighborhood know it. The relatives I have left know it. You are not staying here. You can't stay with me!"

At that time, there was a bench where all the men went around the corner. So I told him to go over there. I tried to talk him out of it for an hour. And he kept saying he was gonna stay with me.

Cop car goes by and they don't stop. I couldn't believe it! So this went on for a while, finally I ended up pushing the guy off of me. I got rid of him. He came after me. I got rid of him.

So he won't be bothering you anymore?

That's right.

Week or so later, a nice cop came by to check on me because he knew I was homeless. I told him what happened. He couldn't believe it. So he said he was going to check on it. He came back a little later and stopped and told me, "I found the notes on it. They did write it down. They saw you. They said the reason they didn't stop is because they thought you could handle it."

Now? People aren't nice anymore. People just don't care about anything that doesn't concern them anymore. People are becoming amoral. It's like the Bible or something. End times. Chaos. Famine and floods. These are very frightening times.

But all these sins, all of this has been around since the beginning of time. Maybe it's something else now. Maybe it's some kind of virus or something. Perhaps it's something environmental. Science tells us that the viruses change every five years. So new vaccines are needed. You have to develop something new. Maybe the world needs a new vaccine.

Fighting. Fighting to feel safe. That's where it all starts.

There was a time in the 1990s. I was searching for all that self-actualization stuff. And in searching, I found there were lots of friends who didn't support me. So I had to cut away from them, emotionally, in order to grow. Friends were talking about diaper sales, how many teeth their kids had. I was talking about advances in the field of medicine. I was bored. Perhaps they were bored with me. But it was a waste of time. I was different from all the other women. Different from everyone.

My early years? I always go back to thinking about my mom. My mom, she had a little money for a few years, but mostly it went to doctor bills. We were sick for a long time; sore throats, broken arms. Often the money would just go to pay doctors; earaches, eye troubles.

My mother was a waitress. And when the money was good, she worked at George Diamond's. That was a fancy place, a restaurant back in the 1950s and 1960s. Congress and Wabash downtown. One of the fancier places that's gone now.

It was a fabulous place. Although when you walked in, if you weren't prepared, you thought you were in hell because there were all these fireplaces, lots of them. I heard that it went back to the time of royalty when every royal person got their own fireplace.

They had a party for the families at Christmas. Sometimes my mother would let me come and set the tables if I washed my hands real good.

And the bosses didn't like that, but I got to do something for my mother. And I hardly saw her. I was in school all day, and she had to go to work at 3:00, so I hardly ever saw her. So just spending time with her, being able to do something for her. Sometimes I feel like I should have dropped out of school in the third grade, just so I could have been home with my mother.

She told me once that when she was younger she thought of being a nun. That kind of dedication came through in the way she took care of her family. It was just her, a single mother. And society didn't like that at all. So she went through all sorts of hell. Not just the doctor bills; she paid for my sister's wedding on a waitress's wages.

She was remarkable.

I guess I got the caring and the sensitivity I feel from her. Creative ways of dealing with the world; like, for example, I learned from her that sometimes you have to use reverse psychology. We'd all be running around and she'd say, "Okay, I'm glad you're running around because if you go over there, and sit still at that table, my contract says I have to give you cookies. And if you're quiet, oh no!" she'd say. "Then I'll have to give you chocolate milk, too!" And she'd act like she didn't want to do it!

Creativity was a very fortunate thing for me to find. What do I mean by creativity? I'd say it like this: Creativity is something that makes you think of things from different angles so you don't always look at the mistakes you made. You look at other people and see they make mistakes, too. So why should you be so down on yourself?

You seem like a person who really likes ideas. Did that come from school or other places, or a combination?

I liked school when it was a good class or we had a good teacher. But usually I did better on my own. I was fascinated with psychology. Read about all the different theories. I didn't think behavioral psychology was the only way. I thought there was some good in all the theories.

But in school, I mostly relied on myself.

My first memories of school were in third grade. I had a tough year. Must have been a broken arm. And that's the year we were supposed to learn math. And I just couldn't learn it. Made me very down on math.

Then I went to Amundsen High School. It's at Foster and Damen, still there. I dropped out. I was pretty shy. And I was down on myself a lot. I'm not so shy now.

One thing I remember about high school: I got to high school and had an algebra teacher that I loved. Even though I had always hated math, I loved algebra because the teacher was so good. She didn't believe in homework. She thought that if we made mistakes, we should all make them together. So we did all our work together. She told us that if she gave an explanation and went too fast; to raise our hand and tell her. And if the explanation was too slow, we could raise our hand and say, "This is trivial!" She was a lot of fun.

You get a good teacher like that in school, and then it can lead you to have all sorts of ideas on your own.

I had all these ideas. I realized I was really intelligent. But there was no one there to help me out. I wanted the father I never had to take care of me. Society was going one way, and I was going another. So I cried. I really cried when I began to realize all this.

But it was a good turning point. From school, to ideas, to worrying about not having a father, that led me to a turning point.

Instead of worrying about myself—I saw the battle was outside me. Anywhere I look outside of me there is danger. I had what it took inside me. It was the world that was dangerous. Like driving. People in giant cars, talking to their kids, texting, talking on the phone going high speeds: that's danger.

I didn't want to be a politician, but sometimes I feel like I could have been one. I like finding good ideas. I like smooth sailing. I like things to go well for people.

As you speak, I'm hearing a lot about ideas.

Ideas are interesting. Fascinating. I would listen to debate shows on TV. It was fun. I'm the kind of person who can debate both sides and no one would know which one I really believed.

Are you a religious person?

I'm very religious. Not in the Catholic sense like a nun, but close to it. I believe in a calling. But I can't go all the way with the church. The church asks, "Do you believe in being called or do you believe what the church tells you to believe—and I believe in a calling. They don't like that. I also think it's okay to be married. So that knocks me out as a nun.

But I do well, I sense the battle between good and evil. I can sense danger.

I see good in the churches. It needs to blossom. They've neglected unity among themselves though. The churches need to work together instead of knocking each other down.

I listen to Mass on the radio.

That's religion. But what about life on the street? Do you have friends?

There are people I hang out with, but they're not really friends. More like acquaintances. Sometimes I don't really trust them.

This is the sixth time I've been homeless. First time it happened, and I got back inside, everybody said to me, "Society is going to try and get you back there on the street."

I've been on and off living on the street. For a while, I lived in a room up on Winthrop, double coffin rooms. That's what they are like, double coffins; knife fights in the hallways.

When I was staying in the coffin room up on Winthrop, there were bugs coming up, chunks of the ceiling falling on me, garbage in the halls, all the power outages. I was toughing it out. I didn't want to move. But then in July they refused my rent. I was the only one in the building who didn't have a drug or crime problem. But when it came time to go to court, I took all my complaints. I couldn't afford to make copies of all of them, but I took most of them. And the judge says, "I don't care. You don't have any rights here. They told you to get out. You get out."

I was the complainer. And no one cared.

I said, "What about my disability?" He said, "I don't care."

Lauren chooses not to speak on the details of the disability.
And her privacy is respected.
Tell me what it's like on the street when it gets cold.

I'm outside now. It's cold, so I ride the Western bus. But pretty soon, it will be warmer, so I'll go back to my spot at Lincoln and Foster. I used to spend the winters in a donut shop up there. But they don't like homeless people.

Being on the street, there are different kinds of survivors.

There are passive and aggressive survivors. With aggressive survivors, you are always in competition. Whether it's for a spot, the favor of some program director, food. The aggressive survivor feels like you need to be eliminated, and if they can do that—they will. So if you feel weak, they will sense that. They will come after you.

The passive survivor just tries to make it, to get along.

I'm more of a scientific kind of survivor. I try to use a system. I try to think. I spend a lot of time looking for answers in books. Talking with people, I'm always looking for ideas. I like trivia. Trivia gets interesting. It gets funny.

You have to learn how to gauge yourself. How to not get paranoid, but still know what to do if something starts going wrong.

You have to have safe places.

That's why the Common Pantry and the Wednesday Welcome Meal is so important. It's something you can count on. I've been coming here for a while now. You can count on it. It's kinda like a neighborhood.

What's it like being part of a neighborhood?

I know all about neighborhoods. That's how I know that the Common Pantry is like a neighborhood. My family has been in the neighborhood since the 1960s. Everything is familiar. Everyone recognizes you. It's familiar. It's belonging. This is where you shop, where you live.

If you're not part of a neighborhood, then bad things happen.

Neighborhoods, like the Common Pantry, are important.

How would I sum it up? I'm an observer. I end up observing because that's all I can afford.

I hope telling my story helps the Common Pantry. I hope this helps you.

I got a very busy life.

I hope I told you enough interesting things. Maybe you could make a series?

I've got lots more!

RAYMOND
Serving His Country

———

Raymond is no stranger to struggle. For him, there always seems to be a new one, whether it is a small struggle like the broken windshield on his car or a large struggle like navigating through life on his prosthetic legs, the need for on-going surgery and managing the monthly bills.

There are even unseen struggles: all he saw while serving his country still fresh and surfacing from time to time. Yet he is an unmistakable survivor. Crutching into the room, he radiates strength. He begins first with stories of serving his country.

———

I was on a U.S.S. carrier, one of the big boys. We had 3,800 troopers on that boat. The ship never slept. A rotating factory, 24 hours a day. One shift on, then you sleep, and then you're on again, 24 hours a day. The ship never slept.

I was 17 years old. I left Chicago the minute I graduated from high school. Every time you set sail, it was nine months before you hit dock.

We were in Germany, France, and China. Hong Kong comes to mind. San Francisco was beautiful, the hills, the trains. Pretty much everywhere in the world. One thing that's true of every city, you can walk 20 paces and everything will change.

That's even true here. 'Course back in the 1970s it was different. I graduated from Roberto Clemente High School. You know, on the west side of Chicago? From there, I went into the Navy.

In the 1970s, it was all about freedom. Safety. You could walk down the street. Didn't have to worry about somebody coming up beside you and hitting you. Somebody coming up to you with a gun. Late 1970s to middle 1980s, it was a decent world.

Now you have to worry about someone coming around a corner and putting a gun to your head. Or doing something right in front of your face. A whole different world now.

Back in the 1970s, it was sweet. Walk from Irving Park down to Belmont and no one would bother you. Now you're scared to walk from your house to your garage.

Back in the 1970s and 1980s, we were always ready. It was always one foot in and one foot out of a war. Reagan was the president. Anything could change. When we'd go across the ocean, we were never one ship. We were 20 ships.

And when that phone would ring saying *Go!*, we all had to be ready to go.

I was a flight guy on the carrier. I guided the jets off and on the boat. Jets and helicopters. Guided the planes with flashlights. A lot of times it's dark. Just the stars and your flashlights. Landing planes with your flashlights. Worked the cables that kept the planes from sliding right off the side of the boat and into the ocean.

And I watched cables take guys heads off just like that. More than once I saw that. I was on the boat for eight years. I saw four guys completely decapitated. Minute that happens, they take the whole crew off duty. There are 22 of us. All the guys on that one crew. Minute something happens, even if a cable doesn't snap, they take everybody off to try and figure out what went wrong.

They ask: "Was this cable greased?" "Was everybody doing exactly what they were supposed to be doing?"

You're responsible. It's us. Maintenance? That's 9 guys. There's the gunnery, that's 22 guys. There's a sergeant and a captain. There's all of us, there's the guys who do the work. And all of us, every single one of us, we're responsible.

They take us to a restraining area. Medical comes in, a psychiatrist. They check you out. Check all your vitals. Check you from top to bottom because, believe me, when you see stuff like that . . . you get numb. You're scared. And then you're thinking, that's my buddy that happened to.

They asked me to reenlist; I said I couldn't do it.

I did it because I love my country. Everybody lives for something. Some people live for bread, some for water. Everybody needs a purpose. I love this country. This country gives me purpose. This country is worth fighting for.

See, the way we looked at the boat? That's our house. We wanted to make sure it was safe. I got 3,000 guys on a boat—and that makes us all safe. Infrared binoculars that can see through the dark. We had those. And you learn how to move fast.

They offered me schooling. , College. For free. I watched my uncles going through college. It was different back then. It was safe.

But then the scenery changed.

I saw too many people losing lives. Planes crashing. Helicopters going down. It wasn't safe anymore. Things got too dangerous. It was like, we had this prime 1955 Chevy. And you're never gonna have a 1955 Chevy again.

I got out. Went to UIC, got my B.A. in engineering. I had one son. I saw my father, and uncles struggle. My dad was in WW II. I went to college.

My uncle ran the Wheeling airport. He was in the service 29 years. He ran an airport out in the northwest suburbs. One time Ronald Reagan, Air Force One, was coming in. They didn't have the code to land. My Uncle told them no. They landed anyway. And Reagan wanted to know who had told them "No."

So they brought out my uncle and Reagan shook his hand and gave him a plaque for doing what was right.

Army, Air Force, Marines—my family has been in all branches of the service. My uncle is buried in Arlington National Cemetery.

It was a pleasure to add to that tradition.

Now, I got two boys—14 and 15. They get As and Bs in school. I've had a lot of struggles. I'm divorced now. Late 1980s, I had struggles. Went from being a green apple to a rotten apple. So I appreciate the Common Pantry. Been coming here a while.

Family helped. I'm grateful for that. But I got to the point where I couldn't ask for help. I'd come to family gatherings, Easter, bring Easter baskets. Nobody hates each other 'cause we put it all on the table. My uncles, my family. They gave me that respect. They'd say, "Let's talk. Let's go to the restaurant, go to your home, my home." I got that respect.

I was a licensed plumber. Electrician, too. Did it for 10 years. I liked plumbing. Plumbing was plumbing.

All the while I'm trying to get my veterans benefits. It took me four years to get my benefits. I kept fighting. I hired a lawyer, and the lawyer went to some civil rights people, and they put me on national TV, and we showed them all the papers. I'm a veteran. I had to beg. I had to borrow, trying to raise myself out of the sewer lines.

> *Raymond glances down at his prosthetic legs before he speaks again, so fast that you're not sure it really happened. He offers no details, so the listener respects his silence on the subject. And he continues, simply stating facts, a story notable for its total absence of self-pity.*

And it stunk. Four years. And it's not like it's all in my head or something.

So I got a pension. But that doesn't cover everything. Right now, I can't do anything. So that's why I'm here at the Common Pantry.

I've always worked. Now I try to work on a computer. When I work on a computer—memories come back. And I freeze.

PTSS? (Post-traumatic stress syndrome)

Yep, that's it. Sometimes I freeze.

You get scared. My kids are old enough. They know now, when dad freezes, that's it. Unplug the phones. My sons know, get me outside. Get me fresh air. Get me the air that will help me till the freezing stops. Till I wake up again. My sons know what to do when Dad freezes up. They are starting to learn that you can learn from the past. So my sons can help when they stay with me.

It happens a lot. Medication makes it worse. Everybody thinks that 'cause you take tons of medication, that it helps, but it really makes it worse. You gotta learn how to get out of it in your own ways.

I started going to church on the boat. We went to church on the boat. I got fond of learning chapters of the Bible. I take full knowledge of my Lord.

Talking about the PTSS helps. Makes it easier. I really can tell when I'm about to freeze—so I just walk outside. I got a little seat. Out on the back porch of my apartment. Got an umbrella. I get some fresh air.

I got a whole apartment full of books. My ex-wife got the house. I got all the books. You can have the house. I want the books. I got the books. Those I will keep as long as I live. And when my ex-wife goes, my kids will get that house. Doesn't matter because I got the books!

Speaking of books and stories, do you know how well you
tell your story? And what an important story it is? You're
a guy who has served his country. You're an inspiration.
He shakes his head.

No. I'm just a guy who would do anything I could to help.

SUSAN
One Wish

———

"If I had one wish, it would be an apartment."

Susan breaks every stereotypical image of "the poor, homeless, or hungry." Like a rapidly and steadily growing number of Common Pantry clients, she is part of the "new poor." Everything she both needs and wants, she once had: a good, steady job, in her case, two jobs; an apartment; and, of course, food in her refrigerator.

Susan is a recent Common Pantry client who has also attended the Wednesday night Welcome Meal.

She is a friendly, engaging woman not new to the working world, but very new to poverty

She could be anyone's neighbor.

———

I'm living in my car.

Trying to get into a shelter of some sort. Having a really hard time. For women my age with no children—it's hard. Women with children go first. So we're kind of last on the list.

It's very dangerous out on the streets. You have to guess where to park. You're always afraid to lay your head down. You're sleeping in your car. You might think it's safe. But then other people think it's loitering.

You have to know where to park every night. Like the other night, I was over by the Fullerton and Cicero area. I was sleeping in my car, and then suddenly they were randomly going around smashing windows. I got out of there fast.

You're always worried. The stress gets to you, makes you old. You have to worry about things like nutrition, too.

These pantries—they give you what they can. Some of them give a little more—but they have more donations. You're always grateful for what you get. I am very grateful for the Common Pantry, very grateful.

Everybody who knows me is worried about me. I'm a more conservative type. I've always worked, mostly in an office. And I always had money. You're used to being able to go to a movie. Now I can't afford going to McDonald's.

I was an accountant. I did purchasing, importing, exporting, human resources. I was with the company for 16 years. I hired and fired people. Didn't like the HR part. It was harsh. Firing someone feels like you are taking someone's life away from them.

I just recently got laid off, about a year and half ago. I loved my job because I got to use my skills. I got to do what I was good at.

The man who owned the company sold it all to a Chinese company. He was old enough to retire. So everything went to

China. I felt good for him because he got out, but it was bad because I wished he could have sold it to an American company. Every single person lost her job, every single one of us.

Before that I worked at fast-food restaurants, Hallmark cards, retail places. My last job, the big job, I was actually working two jobs. I would go at night and work at an outlet store. For eight years, I worked two jobs. I didn't make a lot. All my savings went to cars, to rent. Just because you have a job, or even two jobs like I did, doesn't mean you can save.

I had a little money when we all got let go. The money, spent some of it on hotels—because I kept thinking things would get better. Nothing like this has ever happened. I just thought it would get better. I was with the company for 16 years.

I am 42 years old. I've always done okay. I just thought things would get better.

Sometimes I can stay with friends. My friends all have kids. A lot of them are losing their places, too. And you can't really depend on friends when they are losing what they have, too. I'll stay with friends for a couple of days, shower, eat, do what I have to do. But other than that—you can't really live there.

What about family?

My mother is still alive—but she's older. And we're kind of on the outs. I have brothers and sisters, but none of them are in Chicago. All of them are out of state.

Chicago? Chicago has changed. I was brought up in Humboldt Park. It was a beautiful, beautiful place. Never had shootings. But it started changing and my parents moved us up to the far northwest side of the city.

I'm Spanish and Swedish-American. Everybody looks at me and says, "You're Polish." But no, I'm Spanish and Swedish. I can speak Spanish, not well, but I can understand it. My mother was from New Mexico. Her father came from Spain. He was a cook. My father was Swedish. He was born in Tennessee. He's also Dutch and Irish. But my father passed away.

I have a brother in Tennessee.

What's it like for you, trying to find work?

It's really hard to look for work when you live in your car. That might be hard for some people to understand, but it's true. I have a cell phone. But it's by minutes.

I'm always moving, so it's hard to find me. And that's not good when you want a job. None of the big stores hire on the spot. It's all online. I use my mother's address. But she doesn't always give me messages.

I stayed with my mother for a while, but we couldn't do it. We couldn't be under the same roof. She had her old-fashioned ways, I had my modern ways. She expected me to have a white picket fence, married, children.

I took the career side. I never had children, never got married. And that disappointed her. But I didn't want to get married just to look good in someone else's eyes. If I ever did get married, I'd want it to be for true love, not for just how it looks.

I tell her, it's my life, Mother. I'm an independent person. A person has her own goals.

My goals? In a year I want my own place and a steady job. That's it. Just enough to be able to live. That's all I want, to be able to go to the movies every now and then. I like the movies a lot. I like Johnny Depp. I've seen him filming on Milwaukee Avenue. He stopped, rolled down the window, and waved.

I'm an independent person. I am an ambitious person. But the way things are now, you can have all the ambition in the world—but it doesn't do you any good. You can be a hard worker, like Me, but if there are no jobs, then ambition and hard work just don't matter.

I'm Catholic. I don't go like I should, but I was brought up Catholic. And that does help me in tough times. It helps you believe that maybe there is a reason for all this.

God is thinking that the world is so full of people being greedy and hateful and he just doesn't want to take it anymore. And maybe God will lead us in the direction to get out of all this.

I'm going in a direction to get myself out of this. If you help yourself, then you are helping others because you are making yourself useful. And then you can be friendlier to others. And then they don't get that attitude back at you. It's a better world.

If I had one wish, it would be an apartment.

CARLOS

A Married Man

———

The expression on Carlos's face says, "There is something I am just about to say."

His hair is streaked with gray. He is often wearing something that says Chicago Cubs. He is always in motion; he never stops. He is always at work. He came to the Common Pantry as a client. He started volunteering, working the only way he knows how: hard, and reliable. Now he's on the staff. As we begin, his phone rings.

The call comes in while we're talking and it's from her, so he answers as if by reflex. Their conversation is fast in the way that only comes when two people are so close that they almost don't need words.

What did the doctor say?
Uh huh . . . okay.

Yeah . . . I know.
Don't forget to bring a bag in the car in case you need it.
See you then.
Me, too.

They had 35 years together.

She didn't just get a cold. She got cancer.

Of course when I lost my job, I lost my insurance. That's when she got sick.

We go to Cook County Hospital. We go there and they say, "No insurance? No job? Then that's good. That means you don't have to pay." So I guess that's a good thing.

You could stick your hand out and touch somebody that had cancer: people here, friends, people where I worked, everywhere.

I worked all my life for insurance. I'm 59. I've been working steady since I was 13.

I was a quiet kid, born and raised on Taylor Street. Originally from Taylor and Grand Avenue. Went to Westinghouse High School, 1137 Franklin Boulevard, first year they opened the school. It was an African-American School.

It was sweet. There were two white guys, six Mexicans, three Mexican girls, two white girls, and everybody else was black. But it was the first year for everybody. So we were all in it together. Everybody, everything, was brand spanking new, teachers, principals.

The building was originally a candy factory.

What was your favorite part of school?

I liked auto shop. Don't know why because I didn't like getting dirty. But I was fair at that.

Every year they let you go out and work. I worked at a Volkswagen dealer. I did everything the Volkswagen mechanic did, but I didn't get paid. I got a grade. And we all did piecework. Best piecework was if you pulled out the engine. Four bolts held that engine in place. That was it.

So I worked in this dealership every year. I liked it a lot. Always got straight As. So the last year, the final semester, I walk in. I take the paper to the teacher, everything I had done at the dealership, all of it. And he gave me a B.

I don't know. All As. Guy from the auto place, he recommended me. But that last marking period I came in, I was doing the exact same thing I did every other year, nothing had changed, nothing, except the teacher screwed me out of that and gave me a B.

He never told me why, never told me why. I still don't know.

So after I graduated high school, I worked for International Speedometer for a long time. A company on the near northwest side. It's gone now. I went there, started working on clocks, then speedometers. The Puerto Rican guys taught me to take apart a dash. I look at a dash, I can take it apart. *(Laughs.)* But everybody can take it apart. It's putting it back together that's tough.

But I wanted to be a salesman. So, after that I became a salesman. I didn't like getting dirty. What's the farthest thing from getting dirty? A salesman!

I sold clothes, downtown, State and Randolph. Beautiful Things for Beautiful People, that was the name of the store.

Haven't been downtown in a while. We don't get downtown much anymore at all. We walk around, my wife and I. I go, "Honey, remember this?" She goes, "Don't start that!"

We'll go walking around and I'll be saying, "Over here was this store, and across the street there was that bar and . . ."Then of course *(he smiles),* my wife will say, "Oh, are you gonna start with all that again!"

Tom Olesker, he was the guy that owned the store. Sweetheart of a guy, Jewish guy, he'd give you the shirt off his back. Treated the salesmen just like he treated his sons, no favorites. Nicest guy you ever wanted to meet. You needed money? He'd give you the money. Didn't say, "When are you gonna pay me back?" Because he knew you were gonna pay him back. I was there 10 years.

A long time. I worked downtown for ten years. I managed one of the stores.

Christmas, that was my favorite time of year. It was packed, always packed. I like being busy. I don't like standing around.

We didn't sell mainline clothing. You gotta remember, this was in the 1970s. We sold all the Afro-American clothes: big bell bottoms, orange shirts, leather shirts, the big hats, fly hats. Which was great. I loved it. You dressed up like that every day. Being a short Mexican guy, running the store. *(He laughs again.)*

Downtown was Afro-American, and that's who we sold to. It was perfect. There was no downside.

And then you had all the restaurants, all the bars. Flo's, remember Flo's? It was a corned beef sandwich place. That was my favorite place. First time I ever met a gay guy. What did I know? All the waiters in there were gay. Great place, Flo's. Best corned beef I ever tasted. Great place, Flo's.

Selling clothes, you knew everybody.

One day in walked Yankees, Number Seven . . . what was his name . . . Mickey Mantle? Yeah! Mickey Mantle! Hey, I'm saying to myself, that's Mickey Mantle. He sold clothes, too. He had clothing stores in New York. So he was checking us out. Mickey Mantle!

Is baseball a big part of your life?

I've got a couple of autographs. Some of the Cubs players from back in our day. I never collected them back when we were kids, though. I lived with my grandmother for a while, four doors from the Budweiser sign by Wrigley Field, and we used to go to the games all the time.

My grandmother would say, "Go on all of you, go to the game!" So we'd all stand at the gate, look at the security guard, keep staring at him. We'd just stare at him. Finally, he'd go, "All right, go on in!" I mean no one was going to games in those days. But we went back then. I never got autographs, not like now.

Now I've got a few. Santo, Ron Santo. You ever meet him? Guy has a big heart. Totally, nicest guy you'll ever meet. I've always been a Cubs fan. Could have been a Sox fan. I grew up on Taylor Street!

But then me and my wife got married and we moved up north. All the way up by Edgewater Hospital. All the way from my family. We moved *away*!

We've been married 35 years, 35 years.. I don't even think about it. Maybe that's why it works. *(He stops and reflects.)* Maybe that's why it works . . . no. . . real reason is my wife. That's why it works. My wife is a sweetheart. She's the best.

That's why we moved away from the neighborhood. I was always getting in trouble. We'd play softball. I was in a league. Bunch a guys after a game? You're gonna go out drinking. And, the way young guys are sometimes, we would go out drinking!

We had an empty lot. We had a big old tree. We'd all be over by the tree. And we'd just drink. Going home right after the game? That was not part of the plan.

She'd go to the game, we'd play three to four games in one day. We ended up playing in the police league. After a while, she'd go, "I'm ready to go home."

I'd go, "See ya! I mean you know, we're gonna drink."

So we moved up north. I loved it up North. You can take any bus anywhere. I don't drive. I don't have the patience. I know my limitations. I don't have a temper. I just know my limitations.

So selling clothes. Baseball. And most of all your wife.
What came next after selling clothes?

The limestone place. I worked for Argyle Cut Stone, 6100 Oakton. out in Morton Grove. We cut limestone. You see the trucks.

I spent 22 years at the limestone place. I have a tendency to stick around when I have a job. They had 26 guys working there. Now they have 3. I ran a water saw. How does that fit with not getting dirty? *(He laughs.)* I go to extremes. It was a swing saw. Rubber boots, water saw, it was great. I was by myself and I liked it.

I can get along with anyone. I'm a guy that sits down in the corner and talks to one guy. Gimme my glass of Crown Royal and then leave me alone. I don't like to go to bars 'cause there is always that one guy who wants to fight and he always finds me. And you can't find a good neighborhood bar anymore.

I spent 22 years at the limestone place. I liked the work. Great bunch of guys. We had good insurance. Then we lost our union rep. For some reason he went to jail. Shocking, huh?

After that, they got some new guys in. They couldn't do anything.

Since then? When I'm not here volunteering at the Common Pantry, I'm looking for work. Anything. You go to Target, Kmart, they tell you—we don't do face-to-face. You gotta go online. So you go online. I had one call back, which was Navy Pier for the holiday festival. I get there for the interview an hour early. Other than me, the oldest person in the group was 22. I'm 58.

Next thing I knew, this older African-American gentleman comes in, and we look at each other and we go, whew—thank God. There are two of us old guys! So I do the interview: security check, income tax, fingerprint. So I'm waiting for the call, and it never came.

I called up for the Taste of Chicago. Girl says, "Well, you can fill out an application." I ask her what the odds are of getting something and she says, "Zero." But I filled out the application.

So I went down there. Went to every booth. Gave everybody my resume. Nothing. I went to the Department of Sanitation. Guy there says, "Oh, we might need you after the Fourth (of July)." I go, "You want me for one day? Cleaning out the urinals? I don't care. Whatever you need."

Kids?

I have kids. My son is 32. My daughter is 25. My daughter lives with us. My son lives by Wrigley Field. He's a chef. He worked for Kuma's on Belmont. Then they hired him at Cubby Bear. The economy—it hit restaurants bad.

What about you and the Common Pantry?

The Common Pantry? I been coming here for six months. Somebody told me about it, that I could get food here. And I thought, you know, I really don't want to do that.

I been working all my life. I'm 58. I worked since I was 13. I've never been without a job. I really didn't want anyone to give me anything. That had never happened before. I've always worked for everything I had.

You lose your job, no money, wife gets cancer. So maybe I'll try coming to the Common Pantry, just once.

First person I met here at the Pantry was Nancy. She talked to me. She really did. She listened. She couldn't have been nicer. And Al? He was great. It was the people here. That's what started it. And I've always worked. So I started working here. So I started working, volunteering here.

Tell me what's important about the Common Pantry?

Everybody comes here. Doesn't make a difference who you are or what neighborhood or where you come from. *He pauses.*

What you just said. Everybody comes here. That reminded you of something?

Reminds me of something that happened back when I was 10. This had to be what, around 1961?

Back then, I didn't really even know there were black people till this happened.

Back in the neighborhood? It was Taylor Street, so there are mostly Italians. Mexicans live on this block, black guys on this block, Italians all over.

But you never really knew that. You just knew that everybody had a block. And we all played baseball together. This was back in grammar school.

So one day we were playing baseball together and a cop car pulls up. They pull this one guy over to the car and the cops start beating him up. They just start hitting him, pounding him. He was just one of the guys. He was just playing baseball with us, and then the next thing we all knew was that the cops are just pounding the hell out of him.

So we all went up around the car, all us little kids, and we're shouting at the cops, "What are you doing?"

So my brother says, go get Dad.

And I ran back to the house. My dad was there with five of my uncles. One of my uncles was a lawyer. One worked on pinball machines, one of my uncles worked for the Tribune. They all came running. And they say to the cops, who were still beating this kid, "What are you doing!"

The cops see it's my dad and my uncles and they say, "Either you walk away from this car or we're taking you along with this kid down to the police station!"

Then my one uncle who was a lawyer says, "I'm his lawyer."

That stopped the cops for a minute. The cops say to my Uncle, "Why are you this kids' lawyer?"

My Uncle says, "Because you're putting this kid in the car and you have no reason."

That's when the cop said it. This was 40 years ago and I remember it like it was today. The cop says, "We got all the reason we need. It's because he's black."

What happened next was that they put all three of my uncles in the car. Took all of them downtown. And it feels like it happened today.

I really never knew that kid was black till the cops said that. We had all hung around since forever. We knew you had to be on your block before dark. But that was it. I didn't even know the kid was black till the cop said that!

The Common Pantry is a little bit like that. This isn't just about food here. This is about people, all of us.

I coulda sold drugs. But I'm 58. I coulda gone out and got in trouble. But here I can do something.

I can make a difference. And I didn't think about that at first. But then you come in, you're stocking the shelves. It doesn't seem like you're helping, but you are.

Here's the thing though: it's helping me more.

I'm not the kind of person who wants to give anybody something.

So why am I here?

You know where I get it from? I get it from my wife. Because she's always doing something for someone else, helping someone. One of our friends had knee surgery. So my wife went over, cleaned her house, walked her around the block, made her dinner. That's what she does. And she's always done stuff like that. So I guess I get it from her.

How the hell does she get cancer?

She says to me, "You do something because it's gonna help somebody else."

That's what she says.

And you know what? It makes you feel better. 'Course I say to her *(and he smiles again),* "You are so full of crap!"

Then I come over here to the Pantry, and it turns out she was right!

It also makes you feel better. That's true, too.

I never really said it to anybody before.

But it does make you feel better. And it does make a difference.

165

****

Since the interview, Carlos has become a paid staff member of the Common Pantry, helping to stock and coordinate food distribution on Wednesdays. His wife passed away from cancer. The funeral service was packed. Many of his friends from Common Pantry came to pay their respects.

DAVE
Playing Rough

———

Dave, what's the story of your life?

He laughs. Dave fills the doorway of the room with an athletic grace. He is a big man. His self-confidence is clear. He is good-humored. The first impression one receives of Dave is of a supremely happy man. That's the first impression.

He answers with a winning smile: "Story of my life? Maybe it's I know everything, I just don't know everybody! Yeah, I tell jokes. People like that. I always told jokes."

But then he adds a hint to the fact that first impressions, of anybody, rarely if ever capture even a fraction of a person's story. He says, "All my jokes got a point."

At 59, an African-American man with two arthritic knees from playing college basketball and with a

B.A in sociology, Dave is a walking, wise-cracking,
and insightful storyteller, full of surprises.

———

I had a rough life. Not complaining, just telling the truth.

I'm from Chicago. Originally from Mississippi, Greenville, Mississippi. My father was a bootlegger. That's why they ran us out of Mississippi. I used to take the 20-pound bags of sugar up to the still. Heavy bag when you're eight years old, but I did all right.

Used to make the corn whiskey. Had us an old car. That's how we'd make the runs. An old Packard, he'd tune it up, my father would. We'd go. This was sometime around 1954. So we leave Mississippi and we moved to the west side of Chicago.

What's your first memory of Chicago?

Working. Never was a time I did not work. First job was on the milk truck. Got up in the middle of the night to do that job. This was on Kostner and Ogden. That was where the dairy was. We'd make all the deliveries. Come nine o'clock, they'd run me by the school, I'd jump off the truck. I was late every day.

What were you like as a kid?

As I child, I had friends. Because I always told jokes, girls liked me. I was one of the bad guys. I was a fighter. I don't care how many would jump on me, 18 of them, 1 of me. I was a one-man army.

Gang bangers, they're cowards. Always more of them.

I had six brothers. They was in gangs. I wasn't in a gang. I was TP: territory protected. I didn't believe in gangs. I believed in making money and trying to get a job.

What's the first thing you ever remember wanting?

First thing I ever wanted? I wanted a bike. And I couldn't get a bike. My parents wouldn't buy me a bike. They would clothe me, feed me, but no bike. So I had to make some money. I did it. I made the money. I bought the bike.

What else was important back then?

My mother believed in church. She told me, "If you don't believe in something, you gonna fall for everything." She died when she was young. She was 40. Kidney trouble. I wasn't all that old when she died. But she had values. She taught me values. She taught us all. She had what eight, nine kids? She taught us how to cook, taught us how to take care of ourselves.

On Sunday—you go to church, first thing. Start at 9:00, over by 1:00. Then my mother, she gave out some money for me to go to the show. Go to Riverview, that big amusement park at Western Avenue and Irving Park Road. 'Course that's gone now. Now it's a police station.

I was a basketball player. I made All-American. I can tell you the year, everything. It was basketball and it was music for me. Music? I knew Louis Price. He sang with the Temptations, with the Drifters.

We went to the same church, Louis and I did. His mother had four boys. He would always be singing. At John Marshall High School? There was a talent show. At the basketball games, Louis Price would be singing.

I was a pretty good basketball player, so I didn't go to John Marshall. I went to Providence St. Mel's. I used to go to all the games, all the schools. Friends at other schools, they'd give me tickets. I'd be all over the place. Basketball, all the time.

Walt Frazier, that was my hero. They called him Clyde. That's for Clyde Barrow, like in Bonnie and Clyde. He played rough. I played rough.

So, like I was saying, I played with Providence St. Mel's—took 'em to the state Sweet 16 in 1970. You go ahead and look that up. I was six foot, but I got plenty of rebounds. We played against La Grange (now Lyons Township). They won the championship that year.

I got an offer to come try out down in Houston. I played an inside game. That didn't work out, so I came back home and played at Wright Junior College. In 1972 I played there, and in 1973 we were number one in our division in the country, All-American Junior College. I used to score 30 points a game. I could shoot outside. I had a jumper that was unstoppable.

Play against the big guys inside? I'd be like Clyde—like Walt Frazier. I'd go foot first, elbow second, ball third.

Other coach would say, "Why you all parting the Red Sea for this guy?" They'd say back—-"When this guy fouls. He really fouls!" I played rough. Crazy David, they'd say.

He laughs. They call me crazy? I'd say I don't care!

In 1976 I went down to Florida, University Central Florida. I played for them. Then they wanted me to go play in Spain. I didn't want to go to Spain. We stayed over there 31 days, an exchange program. Flew from Orlando to New York. Then we got a 747 and flew to Barcelona. Took us 14 hours. Then Madrid, all over Spain. International game is different. Rim is different, different game.

But they were cheering for me there. Because I was playing both offense and defense. And they liked the way I played rough. They hadn't seen that before.

Everything's different in Spain. I didn't like it. Stores close in the middle of the day. Drinking goat milk; I hate drinking goat milk. No McDonald's. I ain't eating squid and octopus!

I go to a bullfight. I'm a stupid American, I'm cheering for the bull! They didn't like that at all. But I thought, that was no real fight. That bull, he didn't have a chance.

People watch movies about Chicago. They think it's like Al Capone. In Spain, they called me "Machine Gun."

That was all the talk about Chicago then. Was no real Al Capone. He long gone.

Here's the truth: truth is right now. Now it really is getting bad. Getting dangerous now.

Like this past Sunday? Let me tell you what happened this past Sunday. I go by the South Side, visit my cousin. I get off the bus, and they all shooting! These dumb kids, they just stupid. They got AK-47s, UZIs. They don't understand how to shoot 'em! I'm talking about the recoil on the gun. They lose it. Can't hold it, the recoil. The damn kids got no clue how to shoot the gun!

They got no idea what they got in their hands. And this is shooting going on right in front of me! This is where that little two-year-old girl got shot in the back of that car. Those dumbass kids didn't know *how* to shoot her daddy sitting right next to her. So you got these guns, and you got these dumb kids don't know how to use them!

I told the police, police right there. I said, "Excuse me Officer . . . ," but nothing happens. It keeps going on.

Why is that? Why does all the fighting go on?

Lots of reasons. People think that there is only one reason. They don't know. There are lots of reasons.

What's the one that comes to mind first?

There ain't no more heroes in this city anymore.

Talk about that.

No heroes when it comes to paying for protection. And that's what we're talking about, paying for protection. Lots a people paying for protection. You give me the money, you be safe. That's what I'm sayin'. That's been going on my whole life.

Like my mother always told me growing up, "Count your friends on one hand." Rest of 'em? They pretend to be your friend. For a dollar? They turn on you.

Nowadays? People turn in their mother.

I grew up on the West Side. All my life I stayed on the West Side. But now I stay on the North Side. Lemme tell you why. When I came back from Florida? When I came back from college, that changed things for me. I began to see what was going on here. That was a wakeup call for me. West Side, it's bad. It's not right.

Now I got a place on the North Side. But I was homeless. I was homeless for 10 years, 1995 to 2005. I was out there on the street every day, hustling. On a rainy day, I'd have to find a hallway or something.

What did you do for money?

Every day, getting metal, getting wire, turning it in for cash. Doing whatever I had to do, whatever I had to do to survive. But it's like this: You got all these problems. Everything wrong. So one day I decided I couldn't handle all this myself, so I was gonna turn it over to God. I went back to what my mother had always told me about church. Sometimes you gotta just turn it over to God.

I got on my knees. I prayed to the Lord to fix this for me. I knew he wasn't gonna fix it today. He wasn't gonna fix it tomorrow. I knew he was gonna fix it in his time. But I knew I had to give back to the Lord.

I went into the shelters. I lived in about five or six different shelters. Then I went to this one shelter, Rockwell and Cermak. Man said to me, "You come from the street. You understand these people. You run the shelter for me?" So I started running the shelter. That was me giving back. Guys come in drunk? I say, "You lay down, go to sleep. You give me any trouble? I'm calling the police."

And I did.

I gave back. I ran the shelter for a year and a half. I didn't get paid, but I ran the shelter. There were 60 to 80 guys coming in every night. But I understood them. Man said to me "You can reach these people." I said, I been in the same place they been in. I did the same thing they did. I give them credit.

I had my B.A. in sociology, from Central Florida. I played basketball, but I completed my education. I knew education was important because my mother taught me that. Kids these days, they don't understand. You have to have your education!

And sometimes, your basketball and your education, they come together. Where I graduated? They had alumni that liked the way I played basketball, so they helped me out a little. And there are things you learn in a basketball game that nobody really sees unless you stop and look real hard.

Like what?

Like this: Sometimes during every basketball game, the ref swallows his whistle. What that means is, they stop being a ref and start being a spectator. See that's what you watch for because that's when the ref misses the call.

And when the ref is looking off being a spectator, he stops really looking at me. You understand? He stops looking at me.

So I used to go out there. Take care of business, playing rough. You gotta know when you are being looked at. And when you not being looked at, you play rough.

Your remember Isiah Thomas? His brother, Larry Thomas, played with me. He got some other brothers, too.

What brought you here to the Common Pantry?

I been coming here to the Common Pantry about a year. Friend of mine, Chris, told me about it. Now I just come here once a month. They help me with food, and I appreciate that.

You were on the streets a long time, right? What got you there?

What got me on the streets was that I was this kid who knew everything but didn't know anybody. I knew how to get dressed up for the interview, talk for the interview, but I didn't know anybody. I tried everywhere to find work. Post Office? Tried there for a long time, but I didn't really know no one. I did all the things I was supposed to do, but I didn't really know anyone, not really. People liked me, but I didn't really know anyone.

Even in basketball?

Oh, there is even more to the basketball. I tried out for the Bulls. They had me and Tate Armstrong up for the job. Tate Armstrong got the job. I really was better. I know good. I know bad. And I was good. I think Tate lasted what, a year?

What happened then?

So I kept trying to get work.

Did that take a while?

Long time. Finally got a job at Wilson Jones. Cut the boards, made the books, ran all the machines. Made books by hand. We made the yellow pads of paper, just like the one you writing on. I was there 11 years. 'Course in the end they owed me pension money. I tried to get it on my own, but that didn't work. So I asked around and heard that they would help you with that kind of thing here. Kelly, Matty, David and others helped me write some letters demanding my pension payments based on some statements I had received, and now I'm getting the pension checks. This place, the Common Pantry, it's about more than food. This is a place that helps people with their life.

So after Wilson Jones?

So after Wilson Jones, I'm back on the streets. Same thing, no job. Now it seems like no one has a job either. Even with my education, no job.

I been homeless. I been in the streets.

But I came back. If Obama can go from the outhouse to the White House, then anything can happen.

Happened to me. I came back. I turned it over to the Lord—so that's how.

I tried to make it in bigger jobs—but I didn't know anybody. That's the story of my life. I knew everything; but I didn't know everybody. (Laughs.) Not complaining. Just saying.

I was on the streets, but I made it off the streets. I got a room. I got odd jobs I do. I get by.

Yeah, maybe staying strong, maybe that comes from all that playing basketball. But where it really comes from? Comes from turning everything over to the Lord.

What is it that keeps you in Chicago?

Chicago is a place where anything can happen. I've got my own place now. Little place, but it's all right. And I'm working a bit, so I get by.

I remember. I always remember where I came from though.

Give me a story about where you came from.
He smiles, and the joy of that smile in the moment just
before he's about to tell a story, that joy fills the room.

You want a story? Okay. Listen to this one. You can believe it or you cannot believe it, but I was there. I saw this. I remember, I'm maybe 10, maybe 11. And this story is true.

Like pretty much every story, it took place on the street, on the West Side. I can tell you the four corners of the intersection we was all standing on. I don't lie. I got no reason to lie.

Now I'm not saying I understood this story back when I was a kid, but I know what I saw.

Things were rough. And on this one corner I see all these people round this man, I go over there, too. Man is Dr. King. Martin Luther King. He just standing on that corner. He's talking with all these people. I look across the street. On this other corner, another man. People around him, too. Man is Malcolm X.

What happened then?

Malcolm X, he walks over to Martin Luther King, he say, "Man, you and I. We fighting the same fight. And they gonna kill both of us."

I'm 59 years old. I can remember Malcolm X sayin' that like it was today!

But that ain't the end of the story. Here's what happens next. See there was this other man. This other man, he on the third corner. Like Dr. King and Malcolm X, he had a lot of people around him, too. He had bunch a people round him, too. So the third man is Muhammad Ali.

Muhammad Ali come over to talk with Martin King and Malcolm X. Dr. King and Malcolm X, they see him coming, they see Muhammad Ali coming over, and you know what Martin King and Malcolm X do? They don't say a word. They didn't even talk to him.

They nod at Muhammad Ali, and then they all move along. Don't say a word to him. Pretty near acted like the greatest fighter that ever was, wasn't even there. Shut him down cold but not even talking to him.

Why'd they do that Dave?

It's the west side of Chicago. Place you got to play rough.

GERALD
His Moment

——

Gerald says, "So the only moment I have is this moment right now sitting here talking to you. That's all I have. This is it."

In a genteel Southern accent that still rings with dignity despite a personal journey through hell, Gerald sits up straight, looks you straight in the eye, and tells his story with the assurance of one who already knows that the act of telling one's story really can be a force for healing. One of 10 children, with a twin brother, he was brought up in Georgia in a Pentecostal tradition.

With closely cropped gray hair, a friendly smile, and casually well-dressed, you could imagine him welcoming you into a small art gallery where his newest work has just gone on display.

——

My bachelor's degree is in Accounting. I lived in Atlanta for most of my adult life. I was raised in Cedartown, Georgia, which is 80 miles north of Atlanta. I moved to Atlanta to go to college in 1980.

I live my life as an open and free gay man. I had a partner. We were together for 21 years. And my partner passed away very suddenly of a massive heart attack. It was in 2004. From there, my life kinda went downhill.

After he died, I came to Chicago for another relationship that I thought would be working out. Me and crystal meth. And of course, you know how that story ends. It did not work out.

I had a good job when I relocated to Chicago. But I was let go, downsizing.

Crystal meth, on the other hand, did not let me go. The worst drug you can get mixed up with; as my counselor told me, it's the drug that's created from hell.

Never tried a drug before in my life. Never had a drug, not once. I didn't start with marijuana or anything like that; I just went straight to the top. And at the top of that list of bad drugs, people usually start out snorting crystal meth and then they slam. Slam, as in using the needle. Not me, I was such an addict, I went straight for the slamming. So I wasn't just addicted, I was addicted to crystal meth, and I'm slamming. I got addicted to crystal meth. Crystal meth was my relationship.

I do things in a big way, even now. When I go to the store and I see something that I want, I can't have just one. I have to have two.

Crystal meth is so prevalent in the gay world. And a lot of people don't know this, but you don't have to even have money to get crystal meth in the gay world. All I have to do is walk up Halsted Street and I'll have a needle in my arm in 30 minutes or less. I just need to cruise another man and I'll be all set. Then I am all set. I'm off to the races.

I began to hit bottom when I woke up one day and I was living at the residential shelter over on Lawrence, near Broadway. I'd been staying there off and on between highs, sleeping there when I couldn't go on the Internet and find a trick that would have me over.

Then I had to leave the shelter. They have a lottery over there to see who gets a bed because they don't have enough beds. And I lost. So I found myself on the street. I stayed on the street for two nights. I found myself homeless. It was 17 below zero.

And I guess, that's when I had my epiphany that, you know, something is not working in your life. You are better than this.

You gotta fall in love with you again. I was in love with someone else for all those years. I was loved back, but I really didn't know how to love me because I gave all my energies to someone else. You know what I mean?

That's when someone on the street told me about Lakeshore Hospital. I had heard of this wonderful place that had a gay and lesbian unit at a hospital. It's called the "La-Ho." It's specific for gay and lesbians that are addicted to crystal meth.

And that's when I went to Lakeshore Hospital. The minute I walked in the door I said "I think I've overdosed on crystal meth." Well they went crazy, you know, 'cause they didn't know whether I was gonna die in a minute or anything.

So they admitted me into the hospital. I stayed for three and a half weeks that first time. I stayed for four weeks the second time. I stayed for five weeks the third time. The fourth time was for another five weeks. This was over a two year period.

And the fifth time—it was seven weeks. That was in 2008, October 2008. The fifth time was my last time. I was then clean and sober. It took me five tries. And I have been clean and sober ever since. The good thing about me coming to Chicago is that I got clean in Chicago.

I do live at the YMCA in Lakeview. I found the place there, my counselor found the place. Keep in mind—I have no income. I had no bed. When I went to the Lakeview YMCA it looked like Buckingham Palace because I'd been staying at the shelter.

Still, it's a great place for me. It's a stepping-stone for me. I don't intend to spend the rest of my life there. There's some people been there 35, 40 years. I don't plan to be there 35, 40 years. It's a stepping-stone. And I can do better for myself.

I'm clean, but still struggle every day with my addiction. But I now know how, how to take that thought, that addiction thought, and turn it.

I know how to *not* let that thought come out of my mouth because once that thought comes out of my mouth it becomes my action. Once I entertain that thought is where I get in trouble. I have to learn to not entertain the thought and replace it with something else that's more positive, Replacing the addiction thought with something that's more positive.

I heard about the Common Pantry here through the YMCA. Because for the last few years I've tried to get jobs, but I've not had any success. I can't even get a job at McDonald's because there aren't any jobs.

So I've been living off of pantries, which I'm very thankful for. I'm very grateful for all I've received from the Common Pantry. I did, just recently, get food stamps, get approved for food stamps, which I'm very grateful for. But Pantries have been what I've lived off of, while I've tried to get a job, over the past three years.

So I'm very grateful for that.

My life today has changed very dramatically. I have a plan for my life because, you know, when you don't have a plan—you plan to fail.

My plan is that every day I get up and I have my morning devotion, first thing. I call it my creator—call it the universe, call it whoever you choose to call it—I call it God. And I ask my God to help me get through that day. And I'm living life on life's terms one day at a time. And that's all I can live. I can't change yesterday because it's the past. And I can't do a thing about tomorrow because it's the future. And I'm not even promised that. So the only moment I have is this moment right now sitting here talking to you. That's all I have. This is it. Whether I want to realize it or not, this is all I have. So my plan is to make it through today. And there's been times when I haven't made it through the whole day, only make it from hour to hour because some days are so tough.

So for those really tough days, I have another plan. In my bag I have a picture of the last time, and I'd be glad to show it to you, of the last time I checked into Lakeshore Hospital.

Gerald reaches down, unzips his bag, and pulls out the picture. It's a gaunt, shrunken-cheeked, and hollow empty-eyed version of the man sitting on the other side of the table.

Every time I think I want to walk up Halsted and put a needle in my arm? I look at this picture and I say to myself, "Do I wanna go back to that?" Do I wanna go back to that life that I was living? This wasn't a life. That was an existence.

One needle to the next. That's over now. Now I have a plan.

****

Since this conversation, Gerald has been able to get an apartment and furnishings of his own with assistance from Common Pantry volunteers and members of Epiphany Church. His apartment is a great source of pride. And he sometimes attends church services at Epiphany.

He has been diagnosed with colon cancer and has undergone chemotherapy and radiation treatments. He has begun to help with food preparation during lunches at the Common Pantry's Common Community.

Estranged from his family in Georgia for 10-plus years, he has reconnected with them and even paid them a visit, paid for by a friend he met volunteering at Common Pantry.

He is still a believer in seeing the value in a moment., still not sure what tomorrow holds.

LEN
Angels in Disguise

Len has so much energy that she seems to be in motion even when she's sitting in a chair. She quickly dispels any notion Common Pantry clients are "all the same." She proves how wrong it is to call Pantry clients "these people" because there is simply no one like Len, no one.

She has already been a featured vendor in StreetWise magazine. Len is proof that the real Common Pantry stories don't start with the Pantry. They start with the people who depend on the Pantry not just for the food, but for a community, a place to belong, a place that will take you in when no one else does.

In this little corner of Chicago, it seems that nearly everything is entwined with Len. Like, for example, the way Len learned to read with her grandmother pointing out signs on the smokestacks and

buildings of the old abandoned movie studio at Irving Park and Western Avenue here in Chicago.

———

I was reading long before I went to school. In fact, I remember coming home crying to my mother, "They're not teaching me about reading! They won't let me read!" We had one of those tiny swimming pools in our backyard, the plastic kind you blow up?

Len ends her description with a question, immediately engaging the listener in the story. With her, every story is a conversation.

You've seen them. There was a swing that hung from the tree. We all loved that tree swing.

And suddenly there is a jump from a backyard pool to a movie studio. Of course the movie studio happened to be right down the street.

The abandoned movie studio was right across the street, the Selig Polyscope Company. Mr. Selig had come out to Chicago from the East Coast with his machine that made silent movies. I believe there might have even been some legal trouble with Thomas Edison. So he built his studio right here at Irving Park and Western. It covered three acres, and 200 people worked there.

The studio, the production company, he eventually moved it from Chicago to the West Coast, to Hollywood, long before I came along. But the buildings were still there when I was three, four years old. Some of them are still there now. The signs were faded, but you could still make out the printing.

In the summers, we'd sit on a blanket in the grass in our backyard. My grandmother would point up at the signs on the smokestacks and the buildings of the old abandoned movie studio at Irving Park and Western Avenue here in Chicago. That's how my grandmother taught me to read.

My grandmother is the one you should be interviewing. God help us, we could bring her back from the dead! In order to really know me, you need to go back and know my grandmother. Maybe she and I were a bit alike?

She came over from Germany when she was 18. Over there, her family lived on "squires land." That meant they were allowed to keep some food from the farming for themselves. They could keep some food, but not much else.

If the squire made a pass at one of the girls, the family moved because my great-grandmother, she would have none of it, none of it.

So as soon as she could, my grandmother came over here to America. She met her first husband here. And he committed suicide. One day he just decided to walk into Lake Michigan. And that was the end of him.

They had one son, Uncle Fred. No one was ever allowed to talk about how his father had died in front of Uncle Fred. Things like that, we didn't talk about things like that. They were so afraid that Uncle Fred would follow in his father's footsteps. Uncle Fred, Fritzie they called him, was very high-strung.

She momentarily retreats to a native German exclamation that roughly translates as "Dear God!"

Ach du lieber. I haven't thought about this in years.

Later on, after her first husband walked into the Lake, my grandmother re-met one of her cousins from Germany who was now here in the United States. This was the man who would be my grandfather. She had always been a little bit in love with him. Now his wife, it turns out, had also died, leaving him alone with three children.

So now my grandmother could marry this man, my grandfather. Soon, my Uncle John was born. (*She laughs.*) He was born a bit early. Then my mother was born.

My grandfather was a bricklayer. He worked over near Addison and Kedzie, where the TV studios for WGN are now. He'd walk to work. And every day my grandmother would send over his lunch.

My grandfather was the kind of man who, when his shirt got dirty, would just throw it in a corner and buy another one. This was of course before he married my grandmother and had a wife to do his laundry. He had a daughter. She did what she could. They lived, he and his three kids, in this tiny basement apartment with a big pile of dirty shirts in the corner.

So much wasn't said in our family. It was the way of the times. Add to that, when the adults talked and didn't want us kids to understand, they spoke German. German was the official language for making sure that kids didn't understand. Now I think back, and I think, "Gee, what was this about?"

Maybe that pile of shirts in the tiny basement was what really got her going on finding the house. Let me tell you about the house. It's the house I live in today.

My grandmother worked for a living. That's where the money came from. She made something like three dollars a week. Which she saved. A good saver.

And one day she spotted a house. For sale for $100. And my Grandma wanted that house.

But in order to get the house, they had to move it because the people that owned the land wanted to clear the space for something else. So in order to move it, they had to chop off the bottom half. They moved houses back then—but they couldn't be too big.

So it became a one-story house with an attic. Of course, that also meant she needed to find land for this house. So she looked over on Byron Street, not too far. And she got the land. All on her own, she did the business.

Then, that same day that the business had all been done, she sent the boys over to the brickyard with my grandfather's lunch for the day, and she told them to tell my grandfather; "Bring home the men on Saturday. I bought us a house. You and the men need to build us a foundation."

Grandma wore the pants in the house.

Yeah, she wore the pants. My grandfather once asked her, "When a couple gets married, who controls the money?" And she answered, "The one who works for it." Women didn't say things like that back then.

Her work? Besides bringing us up and taking care of the house? She started out cleaning homes for rich people. Became a cook, then became a sort of personal assistant to very rich people, like a valet, helping them dress, things like that.

So my mother, just like my grandmother, they were always working. That's what German women do! That's what I did! The number of jobs I've had. The things I've done. We could talk for days!

I was born after the war, 1947. The first eight years of my life were wonderful. I'm a baby boomer.

School? I was not a good kindergartner. Wasn't my thing.

I loved school when I had the right teacher, or the right subject. I know how to think, how to reason. I have discipline. I'm very bright in some areas, not in others. My husband used to say that all it took for me to get lost was to drive the car out of the garage.

I'm German!

She laughs and uses the German phrase for "That is right."

Das ist richtig! I could do brain surgery if you gave me the book of instructions! That's how Germans think. Give us a book and we can do anything, but we need that book!

Like I said before, in my family, German was the preferred language for not letting the kids know what's going on. I knew a little, but not much

I had a pretty quiet childhood, but when I was eight years old, everything changed. I started getting scared, having this fear, this nameless fear. It stayed with me. And I didn't really understand it till much, much later in my life.

What happened? I don't remember which came first. The Grimes sisters murders or the Peterson-Schuessler murders. They were around the same time, the mid 1950s. And when those four kids were murdered? Everything changed. Not just for me or for our family, but Chicago itself changed. Everything was different.

Suddenly we got locks on the doors. We weren't allowed to sleep out in the backyard anymore. And no one told us why. I knew *nothing* of the murders. Two little boys murdered on their way home from a movie. I didn't find out about them till well into the 1990s and the candy heiress Helen Brach was killed. That's when they started writing about the connections between her murder and the murder of the Schuessler and Peterson boys. So as I child of eight, I just knew enough to be scared.

The Grimes sisters, the other big event, no one talked about that either. Two sisters chopped up and put in a keg; to this day, no one really knows the killer. But if the grown-ups talked about it back then—they spoke German.

What scared me is that before this happened, we were allowed to fall asleep in the backyard on a blanket at night. We'd wake up in our beds, but we were allowed to fall asleep on blankets. My grandmother had a swing, a wonderful, creaky swing. No one had locks on their doors. Chicago was a very innocent place. That all changed. Everything was safe; but now, now everything was scary. And I didn't know why.

I was kept away from the news. But I was allowed to read the feature stuff in the newspapers. The advice columnists who came before Dear Abby. That was my job, to read to my grandma. She could read for herself, but she liked it when I would read to her. And we would discuss why this happened, why that happened. We'd talk about it. "She should leave the guy! She should walk away!" This is how you learn what's really important. This is how you learn moral attitudes. You have conversations. I had those conversations with my grandma.

All the fear though, it kind of settled in and stayed. There must have been some kind of reasoning. But I didn't understand it. I was eight. I heard, "Everybody is putting locks on their doors now." That's it.

When it really got scary? I mean when the fear was at its worst? The adults pretended that putting locks on the doors was the "in" thing to do. "Mrs. Somerset bought locks. So I'm buying them." That's what I'd hear.

So I carried that fear around with me even into the time I was a teenager. I was different as a teenager. I was among the first girls to wear pants to Lake View High School. I wanted to be comfortable.

I was a reader as a teenager. I wasn't boy crazy, finishing up with one man going on to the next. If you can't stand on your own two feet? Forget it! All the women in my family? They stood on their own two feet.

You gotta live with yourself before you live with anyone else. I was married 33 years. I married a man who had plenty of faults, but so did I. Which was a good thing because if one of us had been perfect it never would have worked.

As a high school girl? I didn't even go to my prom. I was not terribly disappointed. But I was pissed that the guy I asked didn't come through and go with me. Not only didn't he come through and go with me, he went with a girlfriend of mine.

But I did get to go to the Army-Navy Dance downtown, fancy restaurant at McCormick Place. They called McCormick the hall that would never burn. And of course what happened a few years later? McCormick Place burned to the ground!

It was at Lake View High School that I came to be so gregarious and able to talk. I took a course in speech. Before that course, I really was a wallflower, didn't have a lot of friends. But I liked to read, be on my own. Till I took this course.

What happened in this course was the teacher, Mr. Walsh, he was fantastic. He was very accepting. Mr. Walsh did something other teacher's didn't do: he really taught you to think. How to think about yourself. How to think about people. If I could've bottled what he did, I would've done it. He was that good. I absorbed it by osmosis. When you start with a teacher like this, you can then go on to even teach yourself how to think. He taught me to teach myself to think. That's how good he was.

Of course. you have to have guidelines. You have to have the ability to change. If you're not willing to change, you're never going to get anywhere.

You have to be able to say, "This isn't working." Or even more so, be able to say, "I'm wrong." You have to be able to take responsibility for yourself, something I've not always been able to do. But this teacher helped me with all of that.

What's an example of how he did it? Let me tell you.

I remember this one time I was walking down the third-floor hallway and everyone in the hallway was craning their necks, peering all around at the walls and at the ceiling. *Everyone* was doing this. You looked down the hallway and there was a whole dang hallway of people craning their necks! Staring at the walls and ceilings! No one is looking straight ahead. Maybe a hundred kids or so craning their necks around looking at the walls and ceilings.

So I looked straight ahead. I looked a different direction than the way everyone else was looking. And way, way ahead at the far end of the hallway was Mr. Walsh. Looking up one way, then another. Then doing it again, and again. He had the whole damn hallway looking up and craning their necks, imitating him! He wasn't *saying* anything! He was just getting everyone to do what he was doing.

I thought I would die laughing. A few of us had caught on. He'd peek down and look at us. We'd peek over and look at him. So he'd know that we'd know he was doing this on purpose. But if he hadn't peeked and smiled—no one would have known.

Why did he do it?

He wanted people to learn how *not* to follow the crowd. Now a lot of the kids in the hallway never caught on. But then later on those of us in his class found out about it, so we got it. We learned what the lesson was all about. We talked about who started it, why we did it, what it meant.

And then there was the time I made the speech about making pizza. . . .

We had to give lots of speeches. Bit by bit, I got through it, but I still wasn't comfortable. And then the assignment was you had to explain something to someone else, teach someone how to do something.

And I'm desperate. I'm looking around. I'm talking to my mother about it. And I think, I wonder if I could make a pizza?

Boxed pizza. And I asked Mr. Walsh and he said that would be okay.

At school, I went downstairs to the cafeteria and asked them if they'd cook it once it was made. They said okay. So I wrote out the directions. It was simple enough. Got my little speech ready. I started in. And then suddenly I'm stuck because I realize that I need to keep talking!

Ever seen a cooking show? They have to always keep talking, and I had no idea how to do that. I could speak the directions, but I had no idea how to keep talking in between directions. Mixing the dough, rolling it, I could talk about what I was doing or going to do—but I had these big gaps of space! Remember, I'm German. We know the instructions, we're born with that, but filling the space between the instructions. Ach! We are not so good at that!

Then I had this inspiration. I don't know where or how it came, but it was an inspiration. I started singing,. "O, sole mio!" I can't sing worth a damn. I'm off-key, but I start singing *because I didn't know what else to do.*

I knew that Mr. Walsh expected me to keep my mouth going, and I wasn't going to let him down.

He starts laughing. The kids all start laughing. Everybody's having a good time. We get it done. And everybody applauds! I was so surprised! I was blown away. People applauded.

People applauded. And everybody had a little taste of pizza.

I couldn't tell you what he taught me that got me to do that. It wasn't coming from me. It came from his encouragement. Maybe it was coming from something he'd said down the line about giving a speech and being comfortable.

Well, since that happened? I've never been afraid to talk in front of an audience. You could give me 3,000 people. I could talk.

She laughs.

Might not say anything valuable! But I could talk.

After high school, I got into college, Chicago Teachers College. It's called Northeastern now.

I didn't do well there at all. There are a lot of tools I don't have. There, at college, it was the math and science tools. I never got them.

I took too many heavy-duty courses. There were things, like reading, like public speaking, that I could do better than anyone. But there were things I couldn't do at all.

So I dropped out. Couldn't handle language, math and science. I got a job typing. Guaranty Trust, on Montrose. Good job. Good enough. I could walk to work.

Little bit later I met my husband. There's a story!

I met my husband over a garden. That's my passion. I'm a gardener. I lived with a girlfriend. It was the 1960s. By that time I had gone to Liberty Mutual. I was trained and licensed by the state in insurance. I took the test—it was supposed to be a three-hour test and I finished it in 20 minutes, That's what I mean about being really good in some things and not others. This was a test that licensed you to work for an insurance company. All the men were walking out of the testing room at two and a half, three hours. There were six women and maybe 100 men. We women all finished in the first hour.

So I worked for an insurance company—but my passion is gardening. And that's how I met my husband, Jack, talking over a garden.

There I was, I'm helping my friend with his garden, and here comes Jack, my future husband. He had brought along a bottle of wine. We all had a little wine. Bathtub gin with somebody soaking their dirty feet in it would have tasted better.

So I walk away thinking this guy was a wino. Amazing that we got together at all. He was in the process of getting a divorce so he was hands off. He had kids.

Bit by bit, we got to be friends. We hung out.

And then one day, we were no longer just friends. I wasn't planning on getting married, so we started living together. His kids would come visit, and I'd hide my stuff. He never asked me to. And it wasn't that I thought I was doing anything wrong. I just didn't want to set a precedent for a kid.

I knew that this was the man I was going to be with for the rest of my life. I knew that. So you get the paper.

We were married in Wauconda, Illinois where my mother and father had purchased a place. We were married for 33 years, together for 35. We worked. He had a photo shop. We both drove a truck. He drove a tanker truck that carried airplane fuel. And he taught me how to drive the big rigs. All the way across the country we drove. We worked. We had so many jobs, you could fill a book with them.

Our motto we stole from Alfred Lunt and Lynn Fontanne" "Divorce never. Murder a distinct possibility."

We would look at each other during a big fight and one of us would say, "Divorce never. . . . ," and that's all it took. We'd both break up laughing.

He worked for Channel 11 (WTTW Public TV), electronics engineer. Took pictures, he was a professional photographer. We worked.

And he passed, oh, I don't know, not all that long ago. I already said I was bad with numbers.

So what brings me here to the Common Pantry?

It's the people.

The people from this place? Kelly? Kathy, Mattie? David? All the people here.

I call them my "angels in disguise."

Sometimes I get food. But if I don't, that's okay. Sometimes I bring food, too. At the Common Pantry, there is so much more than the delivery of the food. Of course we all need food. We're people. But there is a way to help people that doesn't make the people feel small. That's what they do here.

That's what my "angels in disguise" do here.

What's your current situation, Len?

I'm joining this church. There are a lot of angels in disguise here. There are folks helping me with my house. It's a really long story, but my utilities are all off. I know there is money, somewhere, money in a bank. But I'm not good with legal stuff. So some folks are helping me with that.

I'm wondering, Len, if you are an angel in disguise yourself Len.

No, I'm the grumpiest giver you ever saw.

But you still give. You're still a friend to everybody you meet.

That's because there's no other choice.

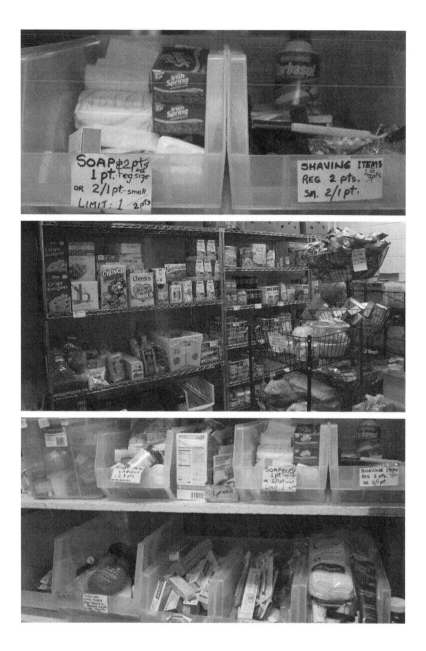

ELVIA
A Faithful Woman

―――

There have always been healers. And there have always been arguments about how to heal. Does healing come from science, from rationality, from faith, or from some combination of them all?

Elvia would tell you that healing comes from faith. From the willingness to believe in larger forces unseen to the human eye.

And it is easy to imagine this twinkling-eyed grandmother as the village healer back in her native Guatemala, back in earlier times.

With a jolly face and dancing black eyes, she is a woman in her 60s who anyone would be proud to call "Grandmother."

Her interview is translated from Spanish by Matty, one of the workers at the Pantry. Her passion for her *family, for her work at the hospital, for the healing she has done, requires no translation. Listen to her story. Decide if you believe everything this neighbor tells you. But as you are making that decision, know one thing for certain: She believes her story.*

———

I have been in Chicago since 1970. I was born in Guatemala. I go back sometimes for vacation time.

My son, daughter-in-law and two granddaughters, we all live in the same building. I have my own apartment, California and Belmont. I take care of my grandbabies.

Nice neighborhood. No problems. Everything has changed since I came. Now it is much more peaceful, quiet.

I am thankful to the Common Pantry. They help people here. They get people through hard times. I have been picking up food for three to four years here. Not every month, but we can come when we need it and they are always here. That is so important. You can count on the Common Pantry.

This place has been a big blessing because this place helps everyone in my house. And everyone is nice to me here. The food from the Pantry feeds my grandbabies.

My son, my daughter, they work. I take my granddaughters to school. Pick them up. I go pick one up right after I leave here. I am home for them.

I worked at Saint Joseph Hospital for 29 years. I started in housekeeping. Later I transferred to transportation, patient transportation. And covering different departments: pharmacy, oxygen, bringing food trays to the patients.

Now I am retired. I retired in 2003. My work now is my granddaughters.

In 1980 I started being very religious. I am Christian. I go to the church. And for me the church is fun. It is joy.

I did not always go to church. Here is why it started: I got separated from my husband, I got divorced. A friend started taking me to church, the Philadelphia Church at Clark and Foster. That started me. I felt the presence of God in my body.

I feel God is with me when I see someone in trouble, and I know I can help that person. This is what I do, I help people because God is with me.

There was a man who had very bad hiccups, four days without stopping. He waited in the hospital for his surgery. But he could have no surgery because of the hiccups; very very bad. I crossed his path with my wheelchair.

I asked him if he spoke Spanish. I asked him what was happening. He was so desperate. He had pulled out his IV. He didn't know what to do; four days he was hiccuping.

I said, "Hold on, I'm going to give you something." So I went and got a small cup of water and handed it to the man. And I said, "Here, drink this. And as you drink this, I'm going to ask God to help you." And as soon as he drank that water, he stopped hiccuping.

I felt it. I felt God. The man was waiting for kidney surgery, but they couldn't do it because of the hiccups. They gave him all kinds of medicine to make him stop. Nothing. No medicine made him stop. But when I gave him the water and I asked God for help—that made the hiccups stop.

I am Christian. I go to the church. Now I go to the New Life Church, on California Avenue. Five services every Sunday, a lot of people. It is God who helps. It is not me.

I don't feel I am a healer. I am very, very faithful. But I am nothing. The glory is from God.

Last year in Guatemala, I met a 30-year-old man who was deported back from the U.S.A. He was very sick. And no one knew what to do with him here in the States. No one *could* help him here. No one *would* help him.

So they sent him back to Guatemala.

He would hit people. He could not control who he'd hit; his arms, his fists, always moving, always punching. No one knew what was wrong. He was a man who just hit people.

So they sent him back to his parents in Guatemala. He had to be restrained—tied up. Every day they had to tie him up.

I was visiting Guatemala. So his parents called me and asked me to come over. "Will you help my son? No one can help him. We don't know what to do. Will you help him?" So I went to the home of his parents. I saw him and told him right away he had to rest. He rested for a while. Then I told him this: He had to say he *wanted* to be better. He had to ask God for forgiveness, to repent.

And the man shouted, "*No!* I don't want to do any of that."

While I spoke to him, his mother held him. So he did not have to be tied down. So, I told the mother to let him go, to let go of him, let him be himself.

And I said to him, "If you don't want to repent—that's okay; God is going to take you anyway. You will die. But it is okay. You will be okay."

I said this, and then I turned around and faced away from him. There was a child outside. Another child. I heard the other child outside cry.

I turned back around to face the young man and he was dead. He was gone. God took him right there. It happened that fast.

One moment I turned away from him to hear the child outside cry, the next moment I turn back and the young man was dead.

Everybody came in. All of them were crying. They said "What did you do?"

But this man who hit people was suffering so very, very bad. All of him was suffering. There was only suffering. Nothing helped him. No one knew how to take care of him. In the time it took for the baby outside to cry, God stopped the man's suffering, God took him. It was very fast.

How was it for you being faithful at the hospital? At your job?

At the hospital, all those years, sometimes it was hard.

I was persecuted for being the faithful one. At the hospital, people would ask me to pray for them. And the supervisors did not like this. It became stressful at the hospital. Patients would hear about me, come seek me out, the supervisors would be angry. They would say, "Do your work!"

Another lady had diabetes. She had lost arms, legs and kidneys. She was in a coma. I told her, "I'm going to pray for you, if you hear me, give me a signal." The doctors were expecting her to die.

So she came out of the coma and she started yelling, "I want to see the lady that prayed for me!!!"

So I got suspended. The supervisors, they did not like the yelling. I was suspended for three days.

The supervisors told me, "We have religious people who see the patients! That is not your job! Get back and do your work!"

I got along with the doctors, the nurses. They asked me to pray for them. The doctors, they say, "Elvia Maria! I have a big operation today! Pray for me!" And they smile.

For me? I have a problem with my thyroid. Sometimes I am hurting. I pray for others and they are healed. I am not healed.

I am a very peaceful person. Before I was religious I was very sad, all my life. But after I found religion, I get very peaceful. My heart is free!

Once I tried to kill myself. I was in depression. But today, I am happy. I am free. I wish everyone was as happy and free as me.

My heart is free!

ROSIE
The Grateful

———

Rosie whooshes into the room more like a force of nature than a person. She is a very proud woman with a unique story. She is all energy. A sturdy, smiling, African American woman, she speaks forcefully and with authority. She has told her story before. She is no nonsense. She sticks to the point and is very clear in everything she says. One would always know where they stand with Rosie.

———

They call me Rosie. I'm 42. I've been coming to the Common Pantry for almost 10 years now.

I was a teenage mom. Living in the Diversey and Damen projects *(Lathrop Homes)* most of my life. Growing up. I had my first son. I graduated from Schurz High School, pregnant and all, going up on the stage. The baby daddy was on drugs.

I had to make something of myself. I had to feed my baby. I had to make ends meet. I didn't know where to go, who to talk to. And someone told me about a Pantry, block of cheese, juices in a box, some cans. But I was grateful. Grateful because I didn't have anything.

Then I got a scholarship to go to nursing school and graduated in 1988. So now I became this nurse. I was still confused. I was 23. My first job was at a nursing home at Diversey and Halsted. I was working there for six years straight.

It was challenging. This was my first time working with elderly people. I'm still staying with my mom. She found out about the pantry at St. Bonaventure. A friend told her. That's how you know. Somebody tells you. That was my first Pantry.

I had no Pampers. My son only had one cloth diaper. The nun said that it was a Pantry so she couldn't do that. Couldn't help me with Pampers. So I begged her.

And she said normally they don't do this—but she's gonna do it for me. So she wrote out a $10 check, gave it to me, and I went to the Jewel on Ashland and bought my son his first box of disposable diapers.

I was so blessed. I was so happy. I told my mom. And she told me—you just have to know your resources.

Then I had my second baby. So my boys were six years apart. I got my first apartment—I was living in the Lathrop Homes. The rent was only $77 a month—but I had to struggle to get it. And now I needed childcare.

Back then, you didn't make money from nursing. I could pay my rent, but finding food was hard. That's where the Pantry comes in. The food to carry me through the month. There wouldn't have been any other way. And I wasn't on public aid. So that's when I started going here regular. I was still working, but there just wasn't enough food. And at the Pantry, there was someone to talk to. They were friends. They understood what it was like.

I remembered that nun at St. Bonaventure. She gave me a blessing. That time she gave me the $10 for the Pampers. I kept saying thank you. Thank you! But the words of my mouth just weren't enough, so I felt I had to do something more. And that's when I started helping out at that Pantry.

I started volunteering on Saturdays and Sundays. Problem was that I didn't have a babysitter. So I told her, "Can I bring my kids?" and she said, "Oh sure!"

I was working. Tired as a dog, but I still made it my way *(Rosie pounds the table as she speaks)* to volunteer for the Pantry. That was my focus. That was something I could give back. For all they did for me, for all I got here at Common Pantry, I could also give something back.

I was still working this whole time, at the nursing home. The old people—-the smell of the chemicals, it was horrible because you have to sterilize everybody all the time. And the smell of the chemicals is like nothing you've ever smelled. Those old people, they are so feisty. A lot of times they fight you when you try and feed them. I remember they would throw trays.

And then you have patients that die on you. And you are close to those people. I had three patients that died on me, *and I was a child*. I was 23, but I was a child.

I didn't understand that the patients died. I thought it was my fault. I didn't turn her right, fix her hair right, feed her right. I thought it was my fault. And they had to tell me, "No, it was just her time to go."

The nursing home was not a bad place. But some of the nurses were bad. I saw them do things like force the patient down, for feeding, changing their diaper. And I thought, that could be *my* mother, *my* grandmother, *my* sister. And I got mad. And I didn't like that. I didn't like that at all. That's what finally made me quit. I couldn't be around that. Six years is a long time. You get a connection with the patients. It's more than a job.

My mother used to tell me, your teachers are like your second mother. You see them for half of the day—and then you come home to me. And that's what it's like being a nurse. You get a connection. I was teaching them how to eat, tie their shoes. They were like my grandparents.

There are four nurses in my family—three aunts and me. I got that down the line. It's in me. It's how I was brought up.

Next place I worked? Worst experience I ever had. I didn't know the language. Most of the people spoke Korean. It was like a different world. I was the new chick. Trying to do everything step by step—they were doing it their way. But it was a physical therapy place. A temporary place. Patients came and went real fast. It just wasn't the job for me. I didn't like the physical therapy part, the way everybody was yelling. I liked to know people. These people just came and went too fast.

So I got a job at Illinois Masonic Hospital. This is 1995. I got into the ER. I loved it. I could make enough money so I could go back to volunteering at the Pantry. I wasn't getting food for myself then. Not at this Pantry or the other one. I didn't need it then. I got on the local school council. I had more time. I didn't need the Pantry for those times. For a long time, I was the volunteer, just giving back.

Then I had the fall.

I was working. I fell. It was my knee, I needed an operation. Another nurse dropped an IV. I didn't see it. I was helping a surgeon. So I slipped, went down, and my knee went out. And the pain was unbelievable. My knee got twice its size, and suddenly I couldn't stand up, so I couldn't work anymore.

I was in the right place for it to happen—cause they took really good care of me. But I couldn't work and that got me depressed. I had always worked. Without working, I didn't know what to do. So I just got depressed.

This was about five years ago. That's when I went on SSI, and so I needed the Pantry again. I am still depressed to this day. I want to do everything myself. I need to take charge, do things my way. And I couldn't do that anymore.

I been coming to this Pantry a long time. You talk about friends? This place is more than the food. These are good people. There is always something here that helps me out.

My son is 23, he's in school. My 17 year old—he's a football player for Lake View. And I have a 9-year-old. She's bipolar.

I am so used to working. The disability benefits help. My son helps a little 'cause he works in the summertime. But the food comes from the Common Pantry. I can make a meal out of nothing. If you got eggs and rice—that's a meal. If you got beans, that's a meal. But it's challenging. And it's hard. I'm proud of that.

When I tell my story, I feel like I'm healing myself. And this isn't even half of it. I got so much to tell. The more I talk about it—the more I tell my kids—the more it's a healing process.

I'm very spiritual. I read my Bible. I look for passages that can help me out. Sometimes I just leave it up to Him. And I tell everyone: You can't take away my joy. I been through so much, but you still can't take away my joy. I try to carry the joy. I'm proud of what I've achieved. My kids have been brought up beautifully. I'm not ashamed to say I go to this Pantry. When I've needed it, it's been there. When I didn't need it, I volunteered.

I'm hoping for my kids, that they'll have it better than me. That they will know they have choices. That they will do to others as others do to them. I want them to have it all. Do everything. I will work again. I love to help people. Private duty nursing . . .maybe I can do that.

I'm a talking person. Hot tea. Quiet. That helps.

This talking? This telling my story? This helped a lot.

FLORA
There Is No Book for This

———

As we speak, Flora dabs a wet tea bag on a blistering burn that circles her wrist like a bracelet. She radiates intelligence, yet almost every piece of her story contains some sort of self-effacing remark. At the time of the interview, Flora was at a low point. She had received emergency assistance from Epiphany Church, and was a regular at both the Wednesday Welcome Meal and the Common Pantry.

She was out of work, out of money, and feeling alone. She was very close to losing her home because she couldn't make mortgage payments and the management and neighbors wanted her evicted because the six dogs living in her condo with her contributed to the uncleanliness of her home.

The story of her successes have often been two steps forward and three steps back. Like many clients of

*the Common Pantry, treating the symptoms at the
surface is helpful but the root cause remains.*

*Eviction and foreclosure were avoided as a result
of scores of hours of volunteer assistance and
persistent "negotiations" with Flora.*

*She listened. Offered help to others in their job
searches. She was there to help when she could.*

*Flora's challenges are not over, but she's also had
her successes.*

———

Flora looks directly at the interviewer and says,

There is no book for this.

No book that tells you how to survive without money. No
directions on how to get food stamps. You go into a Department
of Human Services office, and they don't always know.

There is nothing that prepared me for real life on the street.
Food stamps won't pay for toothpaste. I didn't know that.

I was lucky. I started out with supplies. People that start out
with no supplies are in big trouble. What happens when there
is no money for things like toilet paper? I learned that I could
get a free phone on a TV commercial. That wasn't in any book.

I'm living on the edge. But I prefer it that way because I don't
like to waste money. There is a frugality in my bones. It's in my
blood. I don't like to spend money.

Living on the edge? It's a rush. But it's also depressing.

*She pauses for a moment and then connects the depression
to being late.*

215

I've been late all my life. It's true, it's true. I was born three weeks late. I don't know if I'm depressed or if I don't realize how long things take to do, but I'm always late.

It took me a few months to figure all this out. How to survive. And I'm still learning. You can go from one church to the other. You can get dinner and clothes.

The Wednesday night Welcome Meal here at this church is really nice. I took some home. I'm so grateful for the Common Pantry. But I don't take food every month.

I learn from people on the streets. You can eat at pantries five days a week if you know how and where.

And there is a laundromat on Pulaski that will let you wash clothes because there is nowhere for a lot of people to do that. Of course even if they have a washer and a dryer, you have to worry about buying soap.

> *I hear you have puppies. And I've noticed a lot of the folks have pets. Having pets—for company, to care for, just for fun during hard times—it's important.*

But you can't get dog food. I've been feeding my dogs corn meal. Food stamps will not pay for dog food. So you have to be creative. But there are ways, things you can buy made of food. You look on the labels of fancy dog food, and you see carrots, peas, and certain cuts of meat. I can put all that together in my kitchen.

That's how I got this burn. I was cooking for my dogs. I burned my arm. I was cooking corn meal for my dogs. Pouring it into their bowls. Tannic acid makes the inflammation go down. And it keeps it from hurting. I have puppies. They make me happy. Papillons; toy spaniels.

What else makes me happy?

I like music, I like to read books. I like to watch educational television. I wanted to be a singer. So I took languages. I've been taking languages all my life. I've always sung. But then my voice changed . . . it's age. You know these old sopranos who have a crackle in their voice. You can't control it. It's age. It just happens. Within six months it can happen.

Marilyn Horne, Joan Sutherland: those were my heroes. Marilyn Horne, she was a natural. She had the control. It was easy for her.

I like to go to symphonies, go to operas. I was gonna sign up for Match.com, but I need a haircut. It's been eight months. It's hard to keep my clothes up.

I studied humanities, history, history of religion, University of Chicago.

Jobs are pretty tough now. Real hard to find jobs without being able to use the Internet. And all of the places like Taco Bell, they are regionalized. So you can't walk to a store and get a job in that store. You have to apply online.

I don't even have two dollars to get downtown on the train. I'm trying to sell some stuff I have in my garage. I'm overdrawn at the bank.

How do I keep up hope? Not in religion, I'm not religious anymore.

I grew up Protestant, Lutheran. Lutherans are very supportive because they believe that God lives through all people equally. So they see inspiration in all the people.

I don't believe that anymore. I don't see any personal God that is really active in any individual's life. I think that's wishful thinking, imagination. Which is fine, imagination does great things for people. It inspires people. But I don't believe in it.

I studied Darwin. I look for natural causes. But when you say that in the church, it's heresy.

I haven't given up my personality. Never has happened. I'm not about to. Never will. That's why my father couldn't get along with me.

I can take things pretty calmly. I owed the bank. I didn't panic. Not like my father, he was an accountant.

I got disinherited. Why? Lots of reasons. First, because I stopped going to church. Another reason was that I went looking for my natural mother. I was adopted. I didn't get along with my adopted mother.

And your father?

Never got to go to my father's funeral. When he died, my adopted mother didn't tell me. That's cruel. Not knowing what's going on. That's cruel.

I have no other family.

What about friends?

I met one girl from the Lutheran church. She just lectured me about self-respect, and about working. She had a goal and an objective written on a piece of paper. She told me I had no self-respect. But she had a husband staying at home with kids, so she could go out and work.

What do you think about marriage?

My mother married for money. I always blamed her because she gave up her personality for that. And then she was an unhappy old woman.

At least I have the freedom. I have the freedom. My grandmother told me I would have all these advantages growing

218

up. I understood her. She had to give up her job when she got married.

My grandpa drank. So my grandma was miserable. She died at 55, heart attack. She spent her life doing what she thought she was supposed to do. She thought she had to have family connections. She married for security. But my grandpa didn't make her happy. She had to give up a job that made her happy. She stayed indoors. Didn't even have a car. She used to wait in front of the window till he came home from work. It was like a cage. He liked it that way.

I never wanted to give up my personality. But I am not blaming women who do that, who give up their personality. Because they are living reasonably well. And I am living without money. I have nothing. They have income.

I could have gotten married and then divorced the person and ended up with half the money. But I didn't do that. I did the ethical thing.

Am I glad I did the ethical thing?

Not now because you could marry and then still have the money.

I don't really ever talk about myself. Not like we're doing now. This is the first time I've ever done anything like this.

I think about myself a lot. But usually there's no one to talk to.

Plans? I've been a paralegal. I worked in a law firm library. But there are different types of certifications now. I'm not even sure what they are.

I had a plan. I put my money in the stock market. All my life, the stock market had done well. Lost it all.

I suppose I could go onMatch.com. Maybe that's a plan.

She laughs.

But not if I had to lose my personality!

DENNIS
The Buildings

———

If someone were to tell you that Dennis was the younger brother of the late comedian Rodney Dangerfield, you wouldn't be surprised. He's a big man with smiling eyes who laughs a lot. He punches out his stories with the rhythm of a wizened New York City taxi driver who could get you anywhere you wanted to go. That, and give you the history of the backstreets you'd never seen before.

But, where Dangerfield would be up in front of the room entertaining the crowd, Dennis would be off to the side with maybe a small group or one person, a person would go home that night thinking, "Geez, that Dennis. A good man. I tell you, did he ever have some good stories! Great stories."

First thing the guy says to me is, "Nah . . . I got nothing interesting. No story."

And then the second we go off to the side and start talking, the first thing he says is, "I put up the John Hancock Center." We talk a bit more, and find out that Dennis has not only put up buildings, he's also blown them up. Oh, and when buildings have caught on fire, Dennis has pulled people out of the flames.

———

As Dennis speaks, strains of both the streets of New York and Chicago come through.

Really, nothing all that interesting I can tell you. Born here in Chicago. Raised in Bay Shore, Long Island, New York. That's all built up now. Like suburbs. Changed a lot. Moved back to Chicago when I was 15. Graduated from Tuley High School, 1300 North Claremont. It's a grammar school now, by Division and Western. Roberto Clemente School took it over.

I was an ironworker for a number of years. I put up the John Hancock Center.

It's just ironwork. Not that big a deal. So ah, we carried beams. One guy welded. The other guy bolted it to the center. I put the antennas on top of the building.

No, I never been afraid of heights in my life.

Every day, there were guys would go on a booze run instead of a break run. I guess it calmed their nerves so they could walk around up there without worrying about it. Maybe a little party when we finished it off! No, it was no big thing.

But being up that high? Walking on the beams? No big thing. I just never been afraid of heights. That's all.

I skydived. I did all that good stuff. Skydive? It's fun. I did it in Aurora. They got a big thing out there. Got into it through a friend of mine. To me it's like a whole world in yourself. You're flying around. You're soaring. I'd do it again.

Guy that ran the skydiving place was a cousin of the guy who did fireworks shows, Fourth of July shows, for the city. I was working for this fireworks guy. You probably saw some fireworks I set off!

Fireworks shows or thrill shows. Whatever you want to call it. I did skydiving shows, the lakefront shows in Chicago, all of that. The Army Rangers, 101st Infantry, that's who parachutes into the water. We worked with them.

They'd take us out, throw us on four barges, we'd time 'em all out. They'd start exploding. You'd just sit there out on the barges: BOOM! POW! BAM!

Yeah, I guess it could get a little dangerous sometimes. I saw a few things. Lots of different kinds of fireworks. The big ones with different colors? The ones that would fill the whole sky? They're made out of crepe paper. You put 'em in pipes. Launch 'em out of pipes. And sometimes, there ain't enough powder on the wick, so the thing doesn't fire. Doesn't shoot off. That's what you gotta watch for.

See, if the guy doesn't see that it hasn't shot off, he'll load it again. That means a double explosion. You got two explosions choking at each other. You want the thing to go up. But it don't go up! So instead of going up, they'll go out. Right at you. Everywhere. The explosion is right there on the barge.

I've seen guys who have had to have rolls of crepe paper removed from their backs.

You gotta know what you're doing. I was a fireworks salesman when I was a kid. I ran across a guy, he and his wife, showed me how to blow up buildings.

I'm a pyrotechnician. I explode buildings. You ever see a building fall down on TV? Like in Las Vegas? Instead of coming in and bulldozing, I put the bombs around the building. Then I push it and it goes to the ground. Doesn't go up, it goes down. That's pyro.

I ran around the world with that guy and his wife blowing up buildings. I don't know, 15 or 16 years. I blew up a bunch of casinos in Las Vegas. Just blew 'em into the ground.

Then I become a fireman.

Twenty years I was a fireman. That was different. It's dangerous work, but it's a good job, good pay, lotta time on and off.

Tripp and Irving Park: that's where I worked out of. I got some merits, for rescuing a pregnant lady out of a burning building.

Then another time, I was going to work and I seen a car crashed up against a lamppost. I looked inside and there was a lady delivering a baby. So I started helping her like I had training in this or something! I was yelling, "Push! Push!" Finally the baby came out. It was just she, the baby and I.

Then I called in to work, called the fire department, and the paramedics came out, took her and the baby to the hospital. She was fine.

I was pretty much always working. Time off from being a fireman, I drove a delivery truck for the Chicago Sun-Times. Bought a couple of apartment buildings.

Yeah, I was pretty much always working. Now I don't do nothing. I'm retired. I come here, the Common Pantry, because it's a good place. And quite frankly, I appreciate that.

I been half way round the world. Virgin Islands, Brazil. They're a lot of fun. The Philippines was nice. It was a great job!

Which one?

All of them!

I liked the demolition stuff, blowin' up buildings and the fireworks the best. It's an adrenaline rush.

What's changed in Chicago? The poorness. You'd be surprised how many people out there on the street don't have a dime. You go down to Wacker Drive and they're lying on the ground stacked six deep. Lying on boxes, in tents. I mean, there has always been people who are helpless, who can't take care of themselves, but nothing like it is now.

In a country that can send billions of dollars around the world, they should take care of their home base first. Yeah, it's getting worse. I don't think it's ever going to get better. Year by year, it gets worse. More jobs are being ripped apart. Ya turn around and 2500 people's jobs are gone like that's hot dog money. I always worked. I even worked at Riverview Amusement Park for a while. Ran the Bobs. They called it the Italian Bobs then. All that's gone, just like the jobs are gone.

Even me. I did all right. I retired with two pensions. I get $1,800 a month, but by the time you pay for rent and insurance, that takes you down to not much for food, so I come here. A friend told me about the Common Pantry. It helps a lot. I been coming here for about two years now.

I been married. I was married 25 years. My wife just passed away two years ago. 'Bout the same time I started coming here. Emphysema got her. This place helps. There's two of them like this. One on Wilson and Hermitage, All Saints Church. I go there, too. Then on Friday, there's a church at Marshfield and Byron. They cook behind the church. Church owns the property.

I'm living *The Life of Riley*! (*Laughs.*)

What advice would I give to kids coming up now?

Save your money. Save whatever you got. There is no "it's gonna get better tomorrow." Forget that crap. It's all lies.

The Common Pantry's
"Circles of Leadership"

Perhaps the most important connection between the voices of the 20 Common Pantry clients included in this book is that these 20 "snapshots" are representative of literally thousands of people served over the years.

There are the common themes we touched on in the introduction. There is the unique, personal story told by each individual. And there is the fact that there are legions of other stories in those thousands of people touched by the Common Pantry since its start in 1967.

That same principle holds true of Common Pantry leadership. Toss a stone into the pond of leadership that has guided the Pantry since its inception and you would have ripples of names that would start to bubble up. Donors, board members, leaders, volunteers, friends, contributors, religious and governmental people; you would have a list that would fill at least one more book. All of those are names of people who have been important in making the Common Pantry successful.

That importance is something you can see in action every week. Walk by the Common Pantry and you'll see trucks being unloaded, boxes being broken down, clients being attended to, bags of food being filled, neighborhood security being supplied. Then take the next step. Start asking the people doing the work about themselves. You'll find that working shoulder-to-shoulder, on any given day, could be: the director of the Common Pantry, any number of board members, regular volunteers, donors, neighbors, kids of neighbors, people who just walked by and wondered what all the excitement was about, members of Epiphany Church or neighborhood churches, maybe even elementary or high school kids.

Scott Best, executive director of the Common Pantry, says, "There is no such thing as a typical volunteer here."

There are only these ripples of leadership, all of which connect to a common mission: creating a place to feed hungry neighbors.

So the people from the Common Pantry and Epiphany United Church of Christ in the conversation on leadership that follows are by no means even close to being the full list of leaders who support the Common Pantry.

They are a snapshot. They are here to represent and speak to that common mission shared by all those who have led, all those who have worked with the Common Pantry down through the years.

Conversations with
Volunteers and Workers

What is the Common Pantry?

Scott: When we opened up the basement of the church, we truly became a full service operation (in collaboration with Epiphany). We became a welcoming place instead of simply a place that gives away food. We truly are a Common Community.

Julie: It's a home base. It's kind of like a grounding place. There is a sense of community here. It's consistent. That consistency of having the same staff members is huge. The consistency makes it a safe place, a place where people feel comfortable.

When you think of the Common Pantry from an operational perspective, the nuts and bolts of the way it works, what comes to mind first?

Scott: Personalities—of clients, board members, different volunteers—coming together under one mission.

Specifically on the client side, it's amazing to see the number of friendships, the number of people willing to help us help them, that's something that really catches your eye.

I was unsure what the actual dynamics between all the various people involved would be when I started. And it seems that 99.9% of the time there is a very harmonious relationship.

Every Wednesday, we receive food deliveries. Clients will always want to come out and help us unload. It's great. They get to see what's brought in. But they are ready and willing to physically help us.

On the operational and volunteer management side—if you take the time to meet a volunteer, to give them a tour to explain what goes on, how we operate, why we need to operate, then a volunteer is going to come back and become a consistent volunteer in the future. So first, if I take the time, or a volunteer who has been here for quite a while, takes the time to really invite a new person in—not just throw them into a station and say okay pack these bags, but give them context of where they are, what they're doing, what the history is—they will come back. Second, . . . the secret weapon is Nancy.

Tell me more about that secret weapon, Nancy.

Scott: How can you not want to work with Nancy? She is the face of the Common Pantry. I do the paperwork, I schedule volunteers, I welcome them in, but Nancy is the hook. Once they meet Nancy, it's tough to not come back.

We mesh together well. First when I was a volunteer and ever since I've been an official part of the Common Pantry. I guess the final decisions come to me, any strategic moves we make, come to me—but Nancy is who really makes things happen.

Nancy, what's the key to doing intake at the Common Pantry?

Nancy: I try to treat everyone the same. I don't always . . . if it gets grinding. . . on my nerves. But I try.

I try to be one-on-one with people. You got to pay attention to the people in front of you. I want to give them that honor. They're probably not the happiest troopers being here. So I try to feed in if they have a comment about their personal life. We have some very sad stories . . . some of the gals, I thought they were gonna die, and then they'd come back. They slip back, up and down.

We've had a lot of laughs and a lot of tears. And there are opportunists.

I have an allegiance to the people I serve. There is something in me that says we have to be helping the next guy. I got into it step by step. I'm at a place in my life where I have more time. It makes a difference for me personally. I just know that when I'm not coming to the Pantry, I am wasting time. Here I never waste time.

Nancy, you've been with the Pantry longer than anyone.
Tell me about the changes you've seen.

Nancy: Since Epiphany Church first took on this huge ministry of allowing people to come in here, that is now officially the Common Community part of Common Pantry, this has made a big difference. The magazines, the clothing, the various games, food, coffee, juices: it's a very nice selection. It is having a place!

There are four or five fellas who never get food. They sit over at that table and they love to play cards. Women read magazines. Kids play games.

That has kept the noise down. . . . they are calmed down a lot. Every now and then, somebody gets loud, but the security guards that Epiphany and the Pantry have for all of the serving hours always takes care of that very fast. Those guards are friendly with a lot of the clients, so there is a rapport there now.

Clients help each other. If someone has too much to handle by themselves, someone else will say, "Let me help you carry that."

The economic downturn, that increased our client load. Scott has all the exact numbers, but I'd guess we are up 30 percent, perhaps more.

A lot of the ethnicities have changed. Ten years ago, the majority of clients were African-American, with some Caucasians who had been here for ever and ever. But the Hispanics have really moved in, and now this is major change. We track ethnicities to know what kind of food to order that might be more appealing to a particular ethnicity and to make sure we have volunteers on staff who are bilingual.

Of the newly unemployed . . . most of them are male, clean shaven, well dressed, and it's like, "Wait a minute, why are you here?"

We cannot turn anyone away.

The relationship between Epiphany United Church of Christ and the Common Pantry has been an important one?

Nancy: I have a letter from Brenda thanking me for working here. I won't ever throw that away. (*Note: The late Brenda Wiegelt Fowler was a leader and pillar of the Epiphany Church Congregation for over 50 years.*)

What is it that allows the church and the Pantry to work so well together?

Kathy: We're all here for the same thing. The Wednesday night Welcome Meal hosted by Epiphany Church is attended by many of the folks who are clients of the Common Pantry. We all work together. We all do our best to help each other out. I think many of us feel called to do this work. I know I do. I remember saying to my employer when I was interviewed, "Wednesday afternoon, I need to leave early. I can make the time up however you'd like. But what I do on Wednesdays is something I feel must do."

Nancy, you are a pillar of the Common Pantry, and Kathy, you are a pillar of the Wednesday night Welcome Meal.

Nancy: *(Laughing)* Well, I don't know about that. But I am a pill!

Tell me about opening up the basement of the church.

Julie: The door to Fellowship Hall was closed, and then one day it was open. One day it was open . . . and everything changed.

I'm guessing there was a little more to it than that.

Julie: We previously had the clients waiting in line outside; its freezing cold and here's this big room that was usable. We started talking to people about using it, and the only thing that was a problem was staffing, making sure that the right people were in place to help the clients, making sure there were computers. If you're hungry, chances are that there are other issues.

So I thought, well, I've got two computers. I know two people I can hire to do this and I'll go to the church council and ask if I can try it out on a temporary basis. It was March 2009. I went to the church council and said, "Can we try it out for a couple of months? I'll take care of the staffing, see how it goes and find out whether we can work it into something permanent."

How did you make sure you had the right people in place to help clients? This was a big change, expanding upon Common Pantry's food distribution and collaborating to providing other kinds of help.

Julie: I knew two great people: one who is bilingual; one who is a single mom who knew how to navigate the systems of government to get aid, that kind of stuff. Both of them had different skill sets. Both of them are moms who needed the work. One is a computer expert. They complement each other.

When you started this new initiative up, were there surprises?

Julie: The one thing that surprised me was how the computer table became a listening table. The computers were there to offer a platform of engagement. They were tools to help us work with the clients in navigating government, getting help, writing resumes. But then you start hearing the client stories, and it becomes much more of a listening table. It's a listening table rather than a computer table. People just want someone to talk to, to listen to them, to hear them.

What's it like to work with the clients?

Kelly: We're like the eyes, ears and hands connecting the clients with the rest of the world. People always want to know what's out there.

There's never just one problem. This woman today, she just lost her job, her gas service got turned off, she's got three daughters, and she's been living without hot water for two months. We arranged for a payment plan on the bill, she got calls backs on the resume, she got a part-time job. I didn't see her for six months, but today she came back just to tell me what happened.

We do a lot of financial counseling. I've written out, this is what you make, these are your expenses. It is a good starting point to finding ways to help with the monthly income and expenses.

What do all of you who work here have in common?

Kelly: The leadership —the people who run it; we're all here in the same fishbowl. Anything can happen to anyone. It's not just coming to get food here.

Is there something that all your clients have in common?

Kelly: Every single person who comes here, in order to get their life in order, they do the work. We might help rewrite their resume, but they tell us what to put. It's their life. It's like someone is on your team. One client couldn't get an ID. We gave her phone numbers, directions, but she got the ID, not us.

No one here is afraid of hard work. Once we help them get the information, they will do the work.

I like the people here. For me? I would want this. I would want someone on my team.

A lot of times it's just listening. You just listen. I shut my computer off. Listening to someone, we might be the only person who does that for a client.

Matty: It's different every time. It's what I expected, to help people. I like it. You feel a satisfaction every time you help someone. I help most with DHS (Department of Human Services) stuff. Like if they want to apply for food stamps, child support, medical. That's mostly what I do.

I go online. So they save a trip. They save hours in seeing their case workers. When I do it online, I know that they will send us something to fill out and get an appointment. So we fill it out, and then they get an appointment. And then they just go for the appointment. They don't have to wait. It takes too long if you go and wait.

Does it work?

Sometimes you hit a wall. There is a family I work with from Ecuador. They have five kids. The wife doesn't work. She has five kids. The man works. But DHS doesn't want to give them food stamps. Only one of the kids has been born here. They have been here three years, but the other kids were born in Ecuador. They need to be residents for five years to get food stamps.

So I was calling. My kids go to a school in Pilsen. There is an office of DHS in the school. I go there, take advice from the people in the school. They help me. Finally, I got it. We found a way for all her kids to eat. It took me three months. I went. They went. I just tried to find ways to help. And we did it.

Kelly: When you think about it, most of us are just one or two situations from being here to ask for help. Something happened, maybe a medical problem, but then something else happened. And then there is no money for food.

Why does this place work so well?

Matty: There is a trust. Clients know I will do as much as I can. So they trust me. I know they trust me because I need to have their social security numbers, very personal information. They come, give it to me. I do everything right in front of them, of course.

Given the Common Pantry history as the oldest continually operating food pantry in Chicago, there is all sorts of potential for the future.

Scott: That's not just a distant future. That's right now. A number of clients have become volunteers. First, people are unemployed and they are looking for something useful to do. Once they get a little bit of insight into the Common Pantry, they want to be involved helping us helping them. Then they find work, and they want to help even more.

Tell me more about right now. We're living in tough times.

Julie: What's changed the most in the past year is the number of people we're working with (at the "Listening Table" or "Computer Desk"), the numbers. In the beginning, there were around 20. Now I see sixty. It's tripled; lots of families; lots of kids.

There's not a lot of support around these people . . . a lot more mental health issues than I realized . . . and there aren't a lot of outside services. And the outside services that are there are really scarce. People are really struggling on their own. So I see this place as a place of support. It's a community. A place where they come and get support.

It makes one feel like they can create their life. Like you can do something about your situation and take responsibility. It teaches you leadership skills, finance skills, which a lot of people do *not* have. Budget skills, not knowing how to budget things is huge.

The beauty of this is that it's so simple. Luckily, we have the two reliable staffers, ones who know what they're doing, an open room, two computers, an internet card and some wonderful other volunteers. That's it. It's so simple.

And then it's taking on a life of its own. All of a sudden there's somebody who drops off food for lunch. When we started allowing people into the Fellowship Hall we had some snacks, but now there's lunch and it's more of a mainstay thing. And I love that because I love the sense of community around meals. The sense of community around eating together is huge.

Neighborhood schools and sometimes restaurants take on "sponsorship" of these lunches for Common community and, while that is much appreciated by our clients, it is also a wonderful hands-on experience for the volunteers.

So why do you do this work?

Julie: I do this because I can, because it's the right thing to do. I like it, if I'm having a bad week, my self-esteem is down, I go over there and talk to people, help out for a couple of hours, and that's my therapy. Just connecting with people there is huge.

Everybody there is part of the community and makes it a nice place to come to. I'm a big positive energy person . . . you're serving other people . . . you're trying to create a nice place . . . at night it's a bit more hectic . . . this is a quieter time . . . people are reading magazines, doing puzzles . . . hanging out. It's a place people can come to. What we want to do here is grow organically. Do the right thing. Do what makes sense.

What's the difference between what happens here at the Common Pantry in the afternoons and any other social agency?

Julie: Social agencies try to accomplish something, and all we want to accomplish is a sense of place, of groundedness. For me, if I were living on the street or bouncing around from apartment to apartment, I would want someplace where I could feel grounded, very rock solid. It's in the basement of a church, which is perfect. It's that groundedness. Yes, you want to help them with the computer stuff if they need it, but really, it's a sense of place that I think is really important.

What about numbers? Give us a snapshot of your client base at this moment (December 2010).

Scott: The client base is a healthy mix between current consistent clients coupled with a healthy mix of new clients. We now serve about 1,200 individuals a month. In 2009, we had over 400 new clients. So the increase has been about 25 percent since the economic downturn.

There has been a large increase in Seniors and a large increase in families with children. We are seeing a great deal of working individuals.

How about a final word? How can we sum this all up?

Scott: I remember when I first started, I went home one night and was saying to my fiancée, we had such a great day today. We had 95 people. And we served *all* of them. And she said to me, "A great day is when you don't have anyone." I'm beginning to understand that. And I think opening up the door to the church was a step towards that day when we are able to have helped people in the many ways needed that we run out of clients to serve.

Hunger can be solved. I still believe it. What I want to do on the road to solving that problem is leave this place a little better than when I found it. Maybe have things that I did, processes I put in place, still be here after I'm gone. To make others realize that people in need are just like them. They are their neighbors.

APPENDIX

Common Pantry

The Common Pantry was established in 1967 in Lincoln Park and is Chicago's oldest continuously run food pantry agency. In the late 1960's, the neighborhood was changing and growing numbers of people in the community were in need of food and emergency supplies. This prompted action by several Lincoln Park and Lakeview churches, as members of The Northside Cooperative Ministry (NSCM) joined forces and provide a solution for those in need.

In response, the Common Pantry was founded and first located in St. Paul's Church at 2335 North Orchard Street, Chicago. In the 1970's the pantry moved to St. James Lutheran Church at 2101 N. Fremont Street It provided tremendous support to the community and furthered the mission for over 10 years. In the mid-1980's, the Pantry moved again, this time to Epiphany United Church of Christ at 2008 West Bradley Place, where it remains today.

Food and personal supplies are obtained from Greater Chicago Food Depository (our Food Bank), Food Rescue, food drives and from the community's churches and residents generous donations. We also provide social service referrals and home delivery for disabled clients.

During the past 45 years various volunteers, individuals, board members, and businesses have joined forces to provide clients a helping hand. Many former clients, whose lives have changed for the better, have returned to help others.

Common Pantry is devoted to providing emergency food supplies and personal items to individuals and families in need in our community. We provide food staples, canned goods, groceries, bread, produce, meats and other personal hygiene items to qualifying individuals at no cost.

Common Pantry is the food bank with a difference, offering a unique feature: an award-winning 'client choice' model. Clients are given points and allowed to choose their own food selections... favorite cereals can be chosen based on their child's tastes or sides selected on weekly meal plans. This unique shopping experience makes the Common Pantry special. It returns the human dignity of choice; something many of us take for granted when we visit our local grocery store.

Common Pantry
3744 North Damen Avenue
Chicago, IL 60618
773-327-0553
www.commonpantry.org

Greater Chicago Food Depository

The Greater Chicago Food Depository, Chicago's food bank, is a nonprofit food distribution and training center providing food for hungry people while striving to end hunger in our community. The Food Depository distributes donated and purchased food through a network of 650 pantries, soup kitchens and shelters to 678,000 adults and children in Cook County every year. Last year, the Food Depository distributed 69 million pounds of nonperishable food and fresh produce, dairy products and meat, the equivalent of 145,000 meals every day. The Food Depository's programs and services for children, older adults and the unemployed and underemployed address the root causes of hunger.

Innovative training programs and initiatives developed by the Food Depository also work to provide men, women and children with the tools necessary to break their individual cycles of poverty.

As Chicago's food bank, the Greater Chicago Food Depository is the charitable food distribution hub for Cook County. Located on the Southwest side of the city, the organization's state-of-the-art warehouse distributes food to 650 member soup kitchens, food pantries and shelters. During 2011, the Food Depository distributed more than 66 million pounds of food.

Most of the Food Depository's product donations come in from food retailers and manufacturers that find a convenient, safe and reliable way to channel food to hungry people that might otherwise go to waste. These are products that could be discarded because of production overruns, labeling errors or changes in marketing direction. The National Good Samaritan

Food Donation Act, adopted in 1996, and the Illinois Good Samaritan Act, passed in 1981, provide food donors with protection from liability claims.

Food donated to the Food Depository comes from more than 650 local and national food companies, grocers, foodservice organizations, produce markets and growers. About 600 food drives are also sponsored each year by more than 500 local business, professional and community organizations, schools and churches. Last year, food drives brought in more than 578,000 pounds of food and more than $825,000.

All food donated to the Food Depository is inspected, sorted, repacked and labeled for distribution to agencies by volunteers and employees who operate out of the Food Depository's food bank and training center.

Member agencies arrive at the Food Depository every weekday in vehicles that range from station wagons to vans to large trucks, to pick up food they have ordered from the food bank. In addition, the Food Depository also employs a fleet of vehicles that help to pick up and distribute food throughout Cook County.

Greater Chicago Food Depository
4100 West Ann Lurie Place
Chicago, IL 60632

773-247-FOOD (3663)
www.chicagosfoodbank.org

Feeding America

Feeding America's mission is to feed America's hungry through a nationwide network of member food banks and engage our country in the fight to end hunger.

In order to learn more about the people we serve, Feeding America undertakes extensive studies. The studies provide comprehensive information on the demographic profiles of emergency food clients and the nature and efficacy of local agencies in meeting their food security needs. Our studies go beyond just the statistics and data – it informs our decisions surrounding the operations of getting food to people in need.

Food Banks: Hunger's New Staple

Feeding America's new study, Food Banks: Hunger's New Staple, details the frequency of clients' visits to food pantries. Drawing on data from Feeding America's quadrennial Hunger in America 2010 study, findings from this analysis suggest that families are not only visiting pantries to meet temporary, acute food needs – instead, for the majority of people seeking food assistance, pantries are now a part of households' long term strategies to supplement monthly shortfalls in food. Results of these analyses suggest that families no longer visit "emergency food" sources for temporary relief, but rely on food pantries as a supplemental food source. Seniors, who so often are limited by fixed or no incomes, are shown to be among the most consistent pantry clients.

The analysis for this study involved the use of a pantry frequency question asked of clients surveyed for Hunger in America 2010. Hunger in America 2010 is the largest study of domestic emergency food assistance, providing comprehensive and statistically-valid data on the emergency food distribution system and the people Feeding America serves. The Food Banks: Hunger's New Staple draws on data from more than 61,000 client interviews that were completed for Hunger in America 2010.

Key Findings:

- Emergency vs. Long-Term Strategy: Emergency food from pantries is no longer being used simply to meet temporary acute food needs. A majority of the clients being served by the Feeding America network (54%) have visited a food pantry in six or more months during the past year.
- Seniors: We find that seniors are disproportionately represented among clients visiting pantries in six or months during the prior year. Over half (56%) of elderly clients aged 65+ are recurrent clients, meaning they have used a pantry every month within the past year.

Households that are food secure are more likely to have recurrent clients – those that have used a pantry every month within the past year – than other types of households. Although we cannot state this relationship to be causal in nature, it is preliminary evidence that food pantry use over longer durations may lower the likelihood of food insecurity.

Working Poor

One of the most common misconceptions is the assumption that if someone is hungry, that means they do not have a job and are living on the streets. What most people don't understand is that anyone can experience hunger. It is a silent epidemic that affects

49 million Americans. According to the US Census Bureau, in 2010, 21 million people lived in working-poor families. This translates into nearly 9.6 percent of all American families living below 100 percent of poverty have at least one family member working . In fact, 36 percent of client households served by the Feeding America network have one or more adults working.

Working Poor Facts

- Female-headed households were more than twice as likely to be among the working poor as male-headed households in 2008.
- Among families with at least one member working at least half a year, families with children were 4 times more likely than families without children to live in poverty in 2008.iii
- According to a survey on hunger and homelessness conducted by the United States Conference of Mayors, 88.5% of cities participating in the survey cited unemployment as one of three major causes of hunger in their city.
- Thirty-nine percent of all adults served by Feeding America have completed high school or equivalent degree with no further education beyond high school. ii
- 34 percent of all households served by Feeding America have had to choose between paying for food and paying for medicine or medical care. ii
- Sixty-five percent of working families that received SNAP were single-parent families.

Feeding America
35 East Wacker Drive, Suite 2000
 Chicago, IL 60601
tel: 800.771.2303
www.feedingamerica.org

I Am Your Neighbor

Community

Words by
David R. Brown & Joseph Burt

Music by Joseph Burt
Typesetting by Jeffry Engert

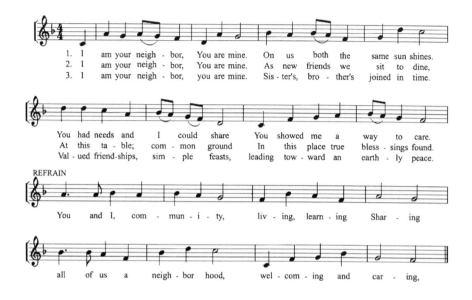

1. I am your neigh - bor, You are mine. On us both the same sun shines.
2. I am your neigh - bor, You are mine. As new friends we sit to dine,
3. I am your neigh - bor, you are mine. Sis - ter's, bro - ther's joined in time.

You had needs and I could share You showed me a way to care.
At this ta - ble; com - mon ground In this place true bless - ings found.
Val - ued friend-ships, sim - ple feasts, leading tow - ward an earth - ly peace.

REFRAIN

You and I, com - mun - i - ty, liv - ing, learn - ing Shar - ing

all of us a neigh - bor hood, wel - com - ing and car - ing,

The hymn "I am Your Neighbor" was written and composed in 2012 in honor of Common Pantry's 45th year of service as Chicago's longest continually-operating food pantry. Common Pantry www.commonpantry.org operates out of the basement, fellowhip hall and kitchen of Epiphany United Church of Christ and serves more than 1,200 individuals from the neighborhood each month. This hymn was first performed at an event officially launching the publishing of a book entitled "I am Your Neighbor" - Voices from a Chicago Food Pantry by David R. Brown and Roger Wright.